THE DOCTRINE OF THE DIVINE INDWELLING

A COMMENTARY ON THE PRAYER OF

SISTER ELIZABETH OF THE TRINITY

The Doctrine of
The Divine Indwelling

A Commentary on the Prayer of

Sister Elizabeth of the Trinity

By

Rev. Mère M. Amabel du Coeur de Jésus
[Carmel de Rochefort]

Translated into English by a Discalced Carmelite

The Newman Press
Westminster, Maryland

1950

Nihil Obstat: Fr Thomas Aquinas a S. Teresia a Jesu Infante, o.d.c.
　　　　　　　Fr Norbertus a Ssmo Sacramento, o.d.c.

Imprimatur: Fr Marcus ab Immaculata Conceptione, o.d.c.
　　　　　　　Provincialis Delegatus. Provincial Anglo-Hibernicae.

21 Maii 1949

Nihil Obstat: Cornelius Lucey
　　　　　　　Censor Deputatus

Imprimatur: ✝ Daniel
　　　　　　　Episcopus Corcagiensis

20 Septembris, 1949

Manufactured by
Universal Lithographers, Inc.
Baltimore 2, Md.
U. S. A.

Te Trina Deitas, Unaque poscimus,
Sic nos Tu visita, sicut Te colimus,
Per Tuas semitas, duc nos quo tendimus
Ad lucem quam inhabitas.

Casa Generaliza
dei
Carmelitani Scalzi
Roma

Rome, March 11th, 1936

VERY REVEREND MOTHER,

It gives me great joy to know that you have prepared a new edition of your excellent book *To Light, to Love, to Life*, and I send you fraternal congratulations—not indeed on account of its popularity from the bookseller's point of view, but because of the good which has already resulted and will result in the world of souls from a work so inspired and so thoroughly Carmelite.

To pray the Prayer of Sister Elizabeth of the Trinity, 'in spirit and in truth', is to practise already her doctrine of faith in the august mystery of the Indwelling of the Three Divine Persons in our soul; it is to penetrate already into that interior spiritual Kingdom where the Trinity dwells; it is to follow in a practical way, Sister Elizabeth's attraction for the true and great life: 'life hidden with Christ in God'.

Your commentary on Sister Elizabeth's Prayer, nourished so thoroughly on the doctrine of our incomparable parents our Mother St Teresa, and our Father St John of the Cross, will greatly help Carmelite souls to know and fathom the practical sense of this sublime Prayer. For you have been well inspired to stress the importance of the ascetic effort which every soul must necessarily make if it wishes, really and not merely superficially, to live the doctrine and follow the way of Sister Elizabeth of the Trinity.

Our Sister, who had intimately experienced 'how much God loves a soul which is self-regardless', after having generously applied herself to this practice of self-forgetfulness has not failed to insist strongly on this point. Now, in order to arrive at this state of self-forgetfulness, one must of necessity practise the theological and moral virtues; otherwise, to pretend to live so elevated a doctrine in the school of Sister Elizabeth would be pure illusion—an illusion all the more dangerous as it would

7

bear on such a vital point of the Christian Life, and would claim as authority and example a soul as deep as Sister Elizabeth of the Trinity. As for Sister Elizabeth, so for all souls without distinction, there is a golden rule to be followed always: the more one desires to approach God by faith and love, the more one must renounce self, forget self, die to self. By following this rule closely the soul will advance safely and rapidly towards Light, Love and Life.

Wishing a wide-spread circulation to your new edition—especially among our Carmels—I beg you, Reverend Mother to accept my devoted and fraternal greetings in Our Lord and Saviour Jesus Christ.

Your Reverence's humble servant and brother,
FR CELESTINE OF ST JOSEPH, O.D.C.
Definitor General

8

PREFACE

THE beautiful doctrine of grace, of the Indwelling of the Blessed Trinity in the just soul, in Christ Jesus, is fundamental in theology. St Paul expressly teaches this, and the early Fathers of the Church, particularly St Augustine, preach the very same truth. The great French School of the XVIIth century, so remarkable in many respects—and so religious, has developed with joy and often with magnificence these same principles of the interior life. There is hardly need to mention the names of Cardinal de Bérulle, the founder, M. Olier, Père de Condren, St John Eudes, and the great Bossuet, whom I would be reluctant to forget.

One must acknowledge that these theses which had never been entirely abandoned, were taken up again during the last fifty years with a new enthusiasm, not only in theological courses but in books destined for the ordinary faithful. Fathers of the Company of Jesus, Carmelites, Dominicans, Franciscans and the Benedictines, have published works both learned and simple—bringing within the reach of all classes the riches of the doctrine of Grace. This has resulted in a wonderful renewal of spiritual life, which has moreover coincided with a renewal of eucharistic devotion—and there may perhaps be between these two facts the relation of cause and effect. It is at least certain that the interior life, prayer, and sanctity, would have derived an appreciable advantage from this outpouring of writings and deepening of fervent life.

In our own days, Sister Elizabeth of the Trinity has grasped this beautiful Pauline doctrine—more than that, she has lived it, and seems to have received from God a special grace to communicate her light and enthusiasm to other souls. So well has she achieved her aim, that, for instructing beginners in the way of the interior life I must say I know of no better book than the life and letters of Sister Elizabeth. Very frequently, this doctrine has given souls a definite orientation towards a life of intimacy with God.

Your desire, Reverend mother, in making use of Sister

Elizabeth's beautiful Prayer—summary of her thoughts and the interior movement of her soul towards the Trinity, is to help your Sisters—and others also—to understand and put into practice this life 'in the Trinity'. To understand it is easy. The difficulty consists in living her faith, in 'realising' these truths, and transmuting them into acts, into prayer, frequent aspirations —carrying these lofty thoughts into our daily duties, however commonplace or monotonous. You will help souls in this, by making meditations easy for them, suggesting thoughts and affections, and often pointing out the practical results of the Prayer on their whole life.

May these pages attain their end! You have insisted on humility, and you have done rightly. Of what use is it to be lifted up by sublime thoughts, if the spirit of pride and selfishness is going to wreck our life of union with God? As the writer of the *Imitation* says: 'What does it profit me to discourse learnedly on the Trinity if I am wanting in humility and displeasing to the Trinity'?

I thank you for the work you have accomplished, and wish it may find many readers—of both sexes. I add one prayer: May all souls who read these pages resolve to make themselves very little—they will understand them better.

And then, I see united the doctrine of your two Sisters: St Thérèse already canonised, Sister Elizabeth who will be perhaps one day (let us not forestall the decisions of Holy Church). We need the little way of St Thérèse and her humility, as the infallible means of becoming like her and like Sister Elizabeth, a praise of glory, a temple of the Trinity, and thus to go to Light, to Love, to Life.

✝ FREDERICK
Archbishop of Sens

8th December 1932

CONTENTS

FOREWORD

THE Prayer of Sister Elizabeth of the Trinity: 'Oh my God, Trinity Whom I adore . . . .' could be made the subject of a complete treatise on the spiritual life. These pages however confine themselves to showing how the doctrine so dear to Sister Elizabeth—doctrine of the Divine Indwelling—perfectly lived by this true daughter of St Teresa and of St John of the Cross, can lead the faithful soul 'to contemplation and to love'— to the union of faith which is the goal of every interior and contemplative life.

It seems, moreover, that Sister Elizabeth's prayer expresses so truly the sentiments and dispositions of soul, characteristic of Carmelites, that it would be profitable to examine it from this standpoint. Hence the practical development of certain parts, especially of the early stages which lead, in some measure into the illuminative way—following the graduation of the prayer itself, before becoming established in the unitive way. Hence also the insistence on the fundamental virtues of humility, charity, and interior silence.*

Each phase then of Sister Elizabeth's prayer, will be only partially developed, according to the inspiration of the moment, in view of the end proposed—sometimes under the form of exclamations or outpourings of the heart—in order to draw from them an invigorating power.

This doctrine of the Indwelling of the Blessed Trinity in the soul—foundation of all spiritual life, belongs essentially to the Order of Carmel: and by the divine inspiration of the Holy Spirit, it has been clearly set forth in the writings of its Reformers St John of the Cross—Doctor of transforming union attained 'in the inmost centre' by means of self-denial and despoliation; and St Teresa—the enlightened guide of the soul in its own 'interior Castle'.

Sister Elizabeth of the Trinity is deeply impregnated with this

*Although these pages are addressed especially to Carmelites, they will prove useful to all souls desirous of leading a perfect and contemplative life: and there are many such, in these days.

13

doctrine. To give full scope to the operation of God's transforming action within her, by constantly setting herself to listen to the voice of her 'Three'—was the aim of her intense interior life. The way by which Sister Elizabeth attained to divine union, taking her stand on this initial ruling thought, was by incessantly returning to the Guests of her soul in a more than ordinary silence and recollection. Active recollection, passive recollection: unshakable determination to close the soul to all that is not God, and powerful grace to do this continually. True disciple as she was of St John of the Cross, in the doctrine of the 'Nescivi', she passed on her way without stopping, in order to arrive at the consummation of love. But while the Doctor of the Nothing insistently places an accent on the 'death' which is necessary in order to ascend, Sister Elizabeth would seem rather to place it on the interior gaze of recollection.

This recollection is of course only practised by means of detachment and death to self, and she knows and teaches this: but she does not stop to analyse this annihilation. She passes as quickly as possible beyond the suffering which it exacts from all the sensitive faculties, in order to concentrate all her powers on loving.

Sister Elizabeth's way will no doubt remain unintelligible for mediocre souls, and perhaps inaccessible to many, owing to its rectilinear movement and its richness. But it cannot fail to attract contemplatives, and it seems specially destined to bring light to truly interior souls. With a remarkable unity she centres all her energies, all her powers, on the effective desire of the 'one thing necessary,' this union of love which is the object of all deep spiritual life.

To attain this union, Sister Elizabeth puts into practical application the doctrine of the Divine Indwelling—doctrine which is *par excellence* simple and unifying: God present in the soul by means of sanctifying grace; and the soul careful to be ever finding Him within, to listen to the interior voice of the Word —forgetting itself in order to give Him full liberty to act in her, and 'to identify her soul with all the movements of His own'. A loving docility to grace, calling for the outpouring of the Holy

14

Spirit's gifts, and through them, the plenitude of the mystical life. It is thus that, with a sustained unity which is truly admirable, and visibly the work of the Holy Spirit, Sr Elizabeth relying on the teaching of St Paul and St John, leads the soul to recollection and to the plenitude of union.

She has proved efficaciously how far into the way of sanctity this 'initial inspiration' can lead if it is fully embraced: intimacy with the Blessed Trinity in the interior of the soul. Her very simple life, reflecting the dominating idea of her spirituality so easily that one can hardly detect in it the least shadow or deviation, is indeed a manifest proof of the strength of this way, leading as it does to the very sources of holiness.

We could have supported our statements in the following commentary by further quotations from St Teresa and St John of the Cross, and other authors who have treated of this question. As our intention was to glorify God in His little *Praise of Glory* we preferred to delve into the rich mine of her own writings, which are always so solid. That is why we have largely drawn on Sister Elizabeth's own thought, as it is expressed in the *Souvenirs* and above all in her *Retreats*.

If we have insisted on the note of peace and joy produced by the union of love attained by means of complete self-immolation, it is in order to re-act against the gloomy dragging of the cross and against the pleasure-seeking tendency which does not want to see in the cross the source of that true happiness, which, under the influence of grace, reigns supreme in every Carmelite soul.

May the *Praise of Glory* obtain from her Three that these humble pages may help souls to find heaven on earth, and that they may fix their dwelling there and radiate God!

On the Feast of the Most Holy Trinity, 1931.

CARMEL DE ROCHEFORT

NOTE: On the doctrine of the Divine Indwelling, apart from the works of St Teresa and St John of the Cross, a number of authors could be cited:

P. Hugon: *L'Inhabitation Divine*.

P. Garrigou-Lagrange : *Christian Perfection & Contemplation*.
The Love of God & the Cross of Jesus.

Cardinal Mercier: *Interior Life.*
Dom Columba Marmion: *Christ the Life of the Soul.*
P. Bernadot: *From Holy Communion to the Blessed Trinity.*
P. de Jaegher S.J. *One with Jesus.*
P. Plus S.J. *God Within us.*
   In Christ Jesus.

        etc., etc.

DOCTRINE OF THE DIVINE INDWELLING

Regnum Dei, intra vos est.

THE doctrine which Sister Elizabeth has brought into prominence is in perfect accord with the teaching of all the great mystical writers—especially with that of St Teresa and St John of the Cross. But as Sister Elizabeth is especially the daughter of her Blessed Father, it is in the works of St John of the Cross that we shall seek the exposition of this fundamental dogma of the Indwelling of the Blessed Trinity, noting briefly the progressive stages of the life of union which it forms in the soul.

St John of the Cross, addressing himself to 'proficients', points out how the initial union of the soul with God present within it, should become ever more intensified, to the point of habitual union and even to the state of union, and the spiritual marriage, which is wrought in faith and in love. His works treat of this mysterious and fruitful ascent which leads to the highest summits which the human soul can ever glimpse while still on earth.

The *Ascent of Mount Carmel* establishes the theological foundation of this initial union: 'It must be known that God dwells and is present substantially in every soul, even in that of the greatest sinner in the world. And this kind of union is ever wrought between God and all the creatures, for in it He is preserving their being: so that, if union of this kind were to fail them, they would at once become annihilated and would cease to be. And so, when we speak of union of the soul with God, we speak, not of this substantial union which is continually being wrought, but of the union and transformation of the soul with God, which is not being wrought continually, but only when there exists that likeness that comes from love; we shall therefore, term this the union of likeness, even as that other union is called, substantial or essential. The former is natural; the latter supernatural. And the latter comes to pass when the two wills—namely that of the soul and that of God—are conformed together in one, and there is naught in the one that is repugnant to the other. And thus, when the soul rids itself totally of that which is repugnant to the Divine Will, and conforms not with it, it is transformed in God

17

through love. This is to be understood of that which is repugnant not only in action, but likewise in habit, so that not only do the voluntary acts of imperfection cease, but the habits of those imperfections, whatever they be, are annihilated . . . . Wherefore God communicates Himself most to that soul that has progressed farthest in love: namely that has its will in closest conformity with the will of God. And the soul that has attained complete conformity and likeness of will is totally united and transformed in God supernaturally . . . . . . If the window be wholly pure and clean, the ray of sunlight will transform it and illumine it in such wise that it will itself seem to be a ray and will give the same light as the ray . . . . . . And the soul is like this window, whereupon is ever beating this Divine Light of the Being of God according to nature, which we have described. In thus allowing God to work in it, the soul is at once illumined and transformed in God, and God communicates to it His supernatural Being, in such wise that it appears to be God Himself, and has all that God Himself has'. (*Ascent*: Bk. II. Ch. V, § 3, 4, 6, 7).

Continuing the exposition of his doctrine in the *Living Flame*, St John of the Cross states precisely: 'In this matter, it is well to note clearly the difference that exists between the possession of God through grace in itself alone, and the possession of Him through union; for the one is a question of mutual love, and the other is one of communication. There is as great a difference between these states as there is between betrothal and marriage. For in betrothal there is only a consent by agreement, and a unity of will between the two parties'. (*Living Flame* St III 24). God has answered the 'yes' of the soul with the true and perfect 'yes' of His grace.

In the *Spiritual Canticle* also, St John continues this subject while expounding his views on the Spiritual Marriage. But he returns first to the fundamental doctrine: 'We must remember that the Word, the Son of God, together with the Father and the Holy Ghost, is hidden, in essence and in presence, in the inmost being of the soul. Wherefore the soul that would find Him must issue forth from all things according to the affection and will,

18

and enter within itself in deepest recollection, so that all things are to it as if they were not'. (*Spiritual Canticle*, St I).

'God then is hidden within the soul, and there the good contemplative must seek Him with love . . . . . thou thyself, oh my soul, art the lodging wherein He dwells, and the closet and hiding place wherein He is hidden. Thus it is a matter of great contentment and joy for thee to see that all thy good and thy hope are so near thee as to be within thee, or to speak more exactly, so near thee that thou canst not be without them, for behold says the Spouse, the Kingdom of God is within you (Luke XVII 21). And His servant St Paul says: ye are the temple of God (2 Corinthians VI 16).

'A great contentment for the soul is it to understand that God is never absent from the soul . . . . . what more desirest thou, oh soul, and what more seekest thou without thyself, since within thyself thou hast thy riches, thy delights, thy satisfaction, thy fullness and thy Kingdom, which is thy Beloved Whom thy soul desires and seeks? Rejoice thou, and be glad in thy inward recollection with Him, since thou hast Him so near. There desire Him, there adore Him, and go thou not to seek Him outside thyself, for so shalt thou be wearied and distracted; and thou shalt neither find Him nor rejoice in Him more surely or more quickly or more intimately than within thyself . . . . .' Hence the necessity for the soul to be hidden also. 'Thus remaining secretly with Him, shalt thou then experience His presence in secret, and shalt love Him and have fruition of Him in secret, and shalt delight in Him in secret—that is to say, beyond all that is attainable by tongue and sense'. (*Ibid.*)

In the second part of the *Canticle* (the illuminative way) St John of the Cross describes what passes in the soul which is accustomed to live in this interior recollection: '. . . . the soul is able to see in that tranquil wisdom, how of all the creatures . . . . each one after its own manner exalts God, since it has God in itself according to its capacity.' (*Sp. Cant.* St. XIV 27). And to attain to the Spiritual Marriage, the soul must needs have 'great strength and a love most sublime for so firm and so close an embrace of God'. (*Sp. Cant.* St. XIX Note).

Finally St John of the Cross describes this 'marriage' of the soul with God, this union of which God is the principle. He 'grants the soul the requisite purity and perfection; for in as much as He transforms the soul into Himself, He makes it to be wholly His, and empties it of all that it possessed and that was alien from God. Wherefore the soul is indeed completely given up to God, reserving naught, not only according to its will, but also according to its works, even as God has given Himself freely to the soul. So these two wills are surrendered, satisfied, and given up the one to the other, so that neither shall fail the other, as in the faithfulness and stability of a betrothal'. (*Sp. Cant.* St XXVII 6) '. . . Therefore, for God to love the soul is for Him to set it, after a certain manner, in Himself, making it equal to Himself, and thus He loves the soul in Himself with the same love wherewith He loves Himself. Wherefore in each of its acts, inasmuch as each is performed in God, the soul merits the love of God, because, set as it is in this grace and in this lofty place, it merits God Himself in its every act'. (*Sp. Cant.* St XXXII 6).

We can see now whither this life of the soul in God is leading: this progress in union can be summed up in these few lines of the *Living Flame*—based always on the fundamental dogma of the Divine Indwelling. 'The centre of the soul is God; and when the soul has attained to Him according to the whole capacity of its being, and according to the force of its operation and inclination, it will have reached its last and deepest centre in God, which will be when with all its powers it understands and loves and enjoys God; and so long as it has not attained as far as this, as is the case in this mortal life, wherein the soul cannot attain to God with all its powers, then although it be in this its centre which is God, by grace and by His own communication which He has with it, still inasmuch as it has the power of movement and strength to go farther, and is not satisfied, then, although it may be in the centre, it is nevertheless not in the deepest centre, since it is capable of going to the deepest centre of God. . . . If it attains to the last degree, the love of God will succeed in wounding the soul even in its remotest and deepest centre—that is, in transforming and enlightening it as regards all its being and power and virtue, such as it is capable of receiving, until it be brought into such a state that it appears to be God'. (*Living Flame* St. I 12, 13).

We shall proceed to show how perfectly this was realised in Sister Elizabeth of the Trinity—the little *Praise of Glory* of all the divine gifts.

INTRODUCTION

Induxi vos in terram Carmeli, ut comederetis fructum ejus,
et optima illius (Jer: 2. 7)

WE have been 'predestinated according to the purpose of Him Who worketh all things according to the counsel of His Will, that we may be unto the praise of His Glory'. (*Eph.* 1 12).

'How can we fulfil this great dream of the heart of our God, this immutable desire regarding our souls—in a word, how can we respond to our vocation and become a perfect "praise of the glory" of the most Blessed Trinity? In heaven, every soul is a praise of the glory of the Father, the Son and the Holy Ghost, because each soul is grafted unchangeably in pure love, and lives no longer its own life, but the life of God. Then, as St Paul says, it knows Him as it is known by Him'. (*Souvenirs*).

Here on this earth, every soul may become a 'praise of Glory', and thus begin the office which is destined for it in eternity. By living recollected within its interior heaven, it places itself under the action of the Holy Spirit; its praise will be uninterrupted. If 'it sings and adores perpetually, it is—so to speak—entirely transformed into praise and love, through its passion for the glory of its God'.

Such is the well-known theme of Sister Elizabeth of the Trinity. Every Carmelite will find therein, summarised in a striking synthesis, the principal elements of her vocation to love. For in Carmel, every soul must commence, in faith, through grace, the office which will be hers in eternity: adoration, praise, thanksgiving, glorifying the Blessed Trinity. Every soul must tend towards the union of love, in the degree willed for her by God.[1]

Only by means of this union, will she fully realise her spiritual mission—her invisible apostolate.

It is of the utmost importance to see whither God is leading us and what He expects of us, and to understand the sublimity of our vocation, so as not to fall short of it; to make our sacrifice

[1]'I have found my heaven on earth, for heaven is God, and God is in my soul'. (*Sister Elizabeth of the Trinity*).

23

fruitful, and to render to God the particular glory for which He has instituted Carmel, the Holy Mountain, whose snow-white peak pierces the vastness of the sky. On this summit, souls can only rest in God, *Dominus Deus Exercituum*, for whose honour they fight with the weapons of prayer and penance. Within this 'enclosed garden', the spouse must find His delights. If it is open only towards heaven, it is to invite souls to tend more particularly to divine things.

In Carmel, everything speaks of God, and tends to Him: separating grilles, silent cloisters, the solitary cell, the austere choir—everything suggests recollection and detachment, necessary for a life of intense union. 'By a divine ordinance, the principal end of our Order is contemplation and love of divine things',[2] says the Prologue to the constitution of the Discalced Carmelites. To realise this goal towards which every Carmelite soul is irresistibly drawn, two things are indispensable, namely prayer and penance. 'The Spirit of our Holy Order is first and foremost a spirit of prayer, recollection, calm, peace, silence and solitude—from whence we draw the strength needed in order to carry out with the utmost perfection all the acts pertaining to the active life. Thus we see that the perfection whose source is in the interior life, when actualized, is put to the test; and this involves the second fundamental law of Carmel: mortification. Mortification of our senses, appetites, will and judgement; mortification by day and night, at all times, whether in solitude or in our dealings with our neighbours and our superiors. The more our soul is purified, the more intense our interior life, and the greater our spirit of contemplation, so also will grow a spirit of renunciation, of death to self, which is characteristic of the sons and daughters of St. Teresa of Jesus and St John of the Cross'.[3] Founded on such a spirit, Carmel seems indeed to have been instituted to keep the torch of contemplation alight in the Church. Has not God Himself inspired its reformers with the luminous doctrine which will ever indicate and shed light on

[2] *'Nostrae vero Religionis . . . . divinitus collatum est, ut potior ejus pars esset, rerum divinarum—contemplatio et amor'.*

[3] *Vie d'Espérance*—P. Servais Mlle de St Ange, o.d.c.

the way to be followed. And as though to confirm solemnly this mission entrusted to Carmel, the church has proclaimed St John of the Cross the 'Mystical Doctor', 'Doctor Mysticus'; and St Teresa 'Mater Spiritualium'.

But if they teach this holy doctrine to all souls, is it not with a special predilection that they point out to the children of Carmel the way to be followed? St Teresa declares this on almost every page of her writings; and St John of the Cross expressly states in the Prologue: 'Nor is my principal intent to address all, but rather certain persons of our sacred Order of Mount Carmel of the primitive observance, both friars and nuns.... to whom God is granting the favour of setting them on the road to this Mount; who, as they are already detached from the temporal things of this world, will better understand the instruction concerning detachment of spirit.'[4] And in order that we may understand and embrace it, we must, by God's grace, desire to be permeated with it—by means of meditation and contemplation, 'watching and praying'—remaining in prayer day and night.[5] That is why 'all of us who wear the holy habit of Carmel are called to prayer and contemplation'.[6]

Is not prayer the essence of our Carmelite life; the very main-spring of its being; if prayer is lacking, all the rest will go astray.

Is it not the source whence the soul derives strength, wherein it drinks of the water of life, and learns to love?.... Prayer makes penance light, because it leads to the effective contemplation of Christ crucified, and in and through this to loving conformity, to the luminous knowledge of Christ glorified.

God has called us 'to be made conformable to the image of His Son.... and whom He predestinated them He also called. And whom He called, them He also justified, them He also glorified'.[7] 'If you be risen with Christ, seek the things that are above where Christ is sitting at the right hand of God. Mind

[4]*Ascent*. Prologue.
[5]Primitive Rule of the Order of Our Blessed Lady of Mt Carmel.
[6]St Teresa. *Way of Perfection*.
[7]Romans VIII 29.

the things that are above, not the things that are upon the earth'.[8]

This is truly the summary of our Carmelite life; total detachment in order to follow the Divine Crucified; understanding of this mystery of death-leading-to-life; losing oneself in the depths of the adorable Trinity: 'To fix our gaze on eternal things, a fruitful gaze leading to love and to efficacious willing—thus becoming established, together with Christ glorified, in the true life, peaceful and luminous—source of all love's victories.' This is the role of contemplation. 'How grand is this life of Carmel! How majestically it is ever descending to us, redolent of the Holy Mountain which gave it birth'.[9]

'The glory of Libanus is given to it, the beauty of Carmel and Saron. They shall see the glory of the Lord and the beauty of our God.... the wilderness shall rejoice and flourish like the lily, it shall bud forth and blossom'.[10] *Sedebit solitarius et tacebit*—He shall sit solitary and be silent'.[11]

Like the great solitaries of former times, we too will establish our soul in God; we will sit down under His shadow, and there remain silent, listening to the voice of the Word. He will teach us all things, and will lead us into this great interior silence wherein the Blessed Trinity dwells. And we shall fix our dwelling there.

In silentio et spe erit fortitudo vestra.[12] In silence and hope shall your strength be. This strength will be given us by our Holy Rule, which helps us to grow in love. Then will our solitude flourish like the lily, and bring forth the flowers and fruits of the Holy Spirit. Then will our life expand in acts of adoration and thanksgiving. It will be as it were the echo of the eternal Sanctus. 'It will sing and adore perpetually, for it will have become, so to speak, all absorbed in praise and love in its passion for the glory of its God'.[13]

[8]Mother Mary of Jesus, of Paray: *Life.*
[9]*Ibid.*
[10]Isaias XXXV.
[11]Jeremias.
[12]Holy Rule.
[13]Sister Elizabeth: *Heaven on Earth* 13th Day.

Zelo zelatus sum pro Domino Deo exercituum.

MARY ELIZABETH CATEZ was born at Bourges, July 18th, 1880. From early childhood, her innocent soul was protected by divine grace, in the shelter of a truly Christian home. When for the first time the child knelt before the sacred tribunal of penance she had a presentiment of the mystery of infinite charity which she was one day to call her 'vision while on earth', and by a divine inspiration she resolved to conquer the defects of her ardent temperament in order to please Him Who was already drawing her to Himself. Hardly had she attained her fourteenth year when she chose Jesus for her only spouse.

Henceforth the way of recollection opened before her—the way which led her to find heaven in the depths of her soul, where in living faith she dwelt united to God. 'It is there I love to seek Him', she would say, 'for He never leaves me. God in me, and I in Him—that is my life'. Through this contact with the Divinity, Elizabeth's soul became enkindled with such a burning love for Jesus Christ that suffering became for her an absolute necessity. At the age of twenty-one, she took flight to the holy mountain of Carmel, whose summit she was to attain so rapidly.

God hid her in the secret of His Face. Sister Elizabeth of the Trinity buried herself in silence and recollection. 'Love dwells within us', she wrote, 'so my sole practice is to enter within myself and lose myself in Those Who are there. The joy of my life is to dwell in intimacy with the Guests of my soul'.

This was for her the secret of sanctity; the form of a continual apostolate, the fruitfulness of which we shall know only in heaven. She compared her role as Carmelite to that of a Priest: 'Both can radiate God and give Him to souls, if they remain always at the divine source.... since Our Lord dwells in our souls His prayer is ours, and I wish to partake of it unceasingly by keeping myself like a little pitcher beside the fountain so that I may communicate His life to others, letting the streams of infinite charity overflow on them'.

Specially dedicated to the Blessed Trinity, Sister Elizabeth longed to be a 'Praise of Glory' to the Three Divine Persons.

This idea, suggested by the Epistles of St Paul, was the keynote of her brief religious life; and she develops it in pages filled with luminous doctrine. For her, it was to begin her heaven on earth: 'Heaven in faith:with suffering and immolation for Him Whom I love'.

The holocaust—long since offered—was to be soon consummated. At the beginning of Lent 1906, God bound His little victim on the altar of sacrifice. 'I am tasting joys hitherto unknown'; she wrote: 'the joys of suffering—how gentle and sweet they are! My soul finds unspeakable happiness in the thought that the Father has predestined me to be made conformable to the image of His Crucified Son'. It was indeed, in the likeness of her crucified Lord, that she passed from this world to her Heavenly Father, on November 9th, 1906. Her dream was realised.

LETTER OF MGR PETIT OF JULLEVILLE, BISHOP OF DIJON, ANNOUNCING THE OPENING OF THE INFORMATIVE PROCESS FOR THE CAUSE OF THE BEATIFICATION OF SISTER ELIZABETH OF THE TRINITY (FEAST OF THE BLESSED TRINITY 1931).

ALMOST a quarter of a century ago, November 9th, 1906, in the Carmelite Monastery of Dijon, occurred the death of a young religious, Sister Elizabeth of the Trinity, in the world Elizabeth Catez. She was twenty-six years of age. She has left behind her a reputation for virtue of an eminent degree—a reputation which, far from fading with the passing of the years, has gone on increasing since her death. It has spread rapidly, not only in France, but in every country where the *Souvenirs*, translated into eight different languages, have been circulated without effort.

Sister Elizabeth of the Trinity attracts particularly those souls who hunger for a deep interior life, for a virile spirituality based upon solid doctrine, and on a courageous faith. Numerous are the faithful, and still more numerous in proportion are the priests and seminarists who love to come and pray at her tomb, and have recourse to her intercession—declaring that they receive through her, graces both spiritual and temporal.

These incontestable facts, have encouraged us to receive

favourably the petition addressed to us by the postulator of this cause, so that the informative process concerning the reputation for sanctity of the Servant of God can be opened. It is indeed important not to let all the witnesses of Sister Elizabeth's life pass away without having gathered their depositions in a canonical manner.

The exhumation of the remains of the Servant of God took place on October 10th, 1930. On opening the grave it was evident that it would be impossible to lift out the coffin which was held fast in the soil by large roots: it was moreover in a very bad condition, and it was necessary to lift out, one by one, the precious bones, which lay on a thick bed of rootlets whereupon the skull had left its impress.... an austere bed indeed, on which it seems as though our venerated Sister had said again in the silence of the tomb: 'O Love, let my substance be all spent for Thy glory'! Everything had in fact been drawn from it by the roots of the great trees, which over this blessed grave sing the glory of God.

The striking spectacle of this total despoliation within the depths of the earth, drew from one of the witnesses this comparison, which came to our minds also: A 'root-like soul'— Sister Elizabeth had in truth been such: losing all trace of self she had drawn from the depths of a life hidden in God, the sap which nourishes the mystical body of Christ, which is the Church. Alone, in the midst of the bones, was found intact and very firm, the little wooden cross which in 1906 had been placed in the hands of her, who like a true spouse of Jesus crucified, had so longed to be transformed into His image.

The remains of the Servant of God were replaced in a little oak coffin lined with white satin, and the precious casket consigned once more to the tomb, awaits under official seal the wise decisions of Holy Church.

May the Blessed Trinity deign to hear the prayers and wishes of so many hearts, and hasten to glorify its Little 'Praise of Glory'.

PRAYER COMPOSED BY SISTER ELIZABETH OF THE TRINITY

OH my God, Trinity Whom I adore! Help me to become

utterly forgetful of self, that I may bury myself in Thee, as changeless and as calm as though my soul were already in eternity. May nothing disturb my peace or draw me out of Thee, Oh my immutable Lord! but may I at every moment penetrate more deeply into the depths of Thy mystery!

Give peace to my soul: make it Thy heaven, Thy cherished dwelling-place, Thy home of rest. Let me never leave Thee there alone, but keep me there, all absorbed in Thee, in living faith, adoring Thee, and wholly yielded up to Thy creative action!

Oh my Christ, Whom I love, crucified by love, fain would I be the bride of Thy Heart: fain would I cover Thee with glory and love Thee, until I die of very love! Yet I realise my weakness and beseech Thee to clothe me with Thyself, to identify my soul with all the movements of Thine Own. Immerse me in Thyself; possess me wholly; substitute Thyself for me that my life may be but a radiance of Thine Own. Enter my soul as Adorer, as Restorer, as Saviour!

Oh Eternal Word, Utterance of my God! I long to pass my life in listening to Thee, to become docile, that I may learn all from Thee. Through all darkness, all privations, all helplessness, I crave to keep Thee ever with me, and to dwell beneath Thy lustrous beams. Oh my beloved Star! so hold me that I cannot wander from Thy light! Oh Consuming Fire! Spirit of Love! descend within me and reproduce in me, as it were, an incarnation of the Word, that I may be to Him another humanity wherein He renews His Mystery!

And Thou, Oh Father, bend down toward Thy poor little creature and overshadow her, beholding in her none other than Thy Beloved Son, in Whom Thou hast set all Thy pleasure.

Oh my 'Three', my All, my Beatitude, Infinite Solitude, Immensity wherein I lose myself! I yield myself to Thee as Thy prey. Bury Thyself in me, that I may be buried in Thee, until I depart to contemplate in Thy Light the abyss of Thy greatness!

'In heaven, I think my mission will be to lead souls to interior recollection, by helping them to go out from themselves in order to adhere to God by a simple, wholly loving movement, and to keep them in this great inner silence which allows God to imprint Himself on them and to transform them into Himself.'

Sister Elizabeth of the Trinity

OH MY GOD, TRINITY WHOM I ADORE[1]

Te invocamus, Te laudamus, Te adoramus, O beata Trinitas!
(Office of the Blessed Trinity)

OH my God, Trinity Whom I adore, help me to forget myself utterly, so that I may be established in Thee, as changeless and as calm as though my soul were already in eternity.

Does not this first cry of Sister Elizabeth of the Trinity voice the prayer of every Carmelite soul who comes to the full realisation of the work which the Holy Spirit longs to carry out in her soul—a work which implies nothing short of the highest perfection?

Oh my God, Trinity Whom I adore!.... Notice at once the intimacy, the spontaneous outburst of a soul that believes and loves. Oh my God—may not every consecrated soul, every Carmelite, say to Thee in truth: 'Thou art my All, my only Good, the One Who dwells within my soul, for Whose sake I have sacrificed all things; my Beloved, to Whom my thoughts revert unceasingly'. He it is Who must help me in all things—above all, in the great work of renunciation and complete self-surrender—so necessary in order to attain to perfection.

Oh my God, Trinity Whom I adore—Truly am I surrendered to Thee alone, Who fillest our cloister and our cells with light and life, 'for without Thee, how empty would they be!'[2] Thee

---

[1] The doctrine of the Divine Indwelling, placing the soul at the very sources of contemplation;—knowledge of God, the First Cause, life of union-of-love—one could have commented Sister Elizabeth's Prayer considered from the innermost centre where God dwells and acts, supernaturalizing at the outset all the powers sentiments and faculties of the creature. As the aim of these pages is to help contemplative souls in general—(or souls called to contemplation)—to understand better how this practice of unceasing recourse to the Divine Presence in the soul, leads surely to true union, it has been judged better to consider each phrase of the text in so far as it admits of practical application—within reach of everyone.

[2] Souvenirs—The references marked 'Souvenirs' or 'Retreat', are taken from the book entitled, *The Praise of Glory*—souvenirs of Sister Elizabeth of the Trinity.

have I desired to find in Carmel, for Thou hast willed to keep me for Thyself alone, making Thy voice so often heard within the depths of my soul, calling me to Thee and reminding me of the demands of Thy love.

To adore—is not that the special and constant duty of a Carmelite, 'wholly recollected in faith, wholly adoring, wholly given up to Thy creative action?'—Is it not the eternal office of the angels, which we commence here below in the heaven of our soul, beneath the light of hope?

Oh my God, Trinity Whom I adore—yes, I adore Thee in spirit and in truth.

Guided by faith, I contemplate Thee in the Holy Eucharist, dwelling for ever in our midst, within the Tabernacle—inviting our silent adoration. I find Thee too in every nook and corner of our beloved monastery, which is irradiated by the light of Thy invisible Presence; in the sheltered garden, where the flowers and birds and insects all speak of Thee and sing in union with all creation a hymn to Thy glory. It is Thee Whom I love in the souls of my sisters—each reflecting one or other of Thy divine perfections, and manifesting Thy gifts. Thee I venerate in authority, coming as it does from Thee and representing Thee. Faith too, shows me in each happening the expression of my heavenly Father's will, and teaches me how to render Thee through every circumstance—joyous or bitter—an ever greater glory, and to gain more graces through the infinite merits of my Saviour Jesus Christ. By faith I follow Thee in every detail of my daily life, marked out with such precision by our Holy Rule under the inspiration of the Holy Spirit. I praise Thee in the trials and sufferings sent me by Thy merciful goodness to goad me on and help me to advance along the narrow pathway ascending the mount of perfection, in that peace and light which streams from Thee.

Faith tells me Thou art ever dwelling in my soul, this little 'house of God'—'the paternal home which we should never leave'—where I would wish to remain united to Thee, always finding Thee, for into this interior sanctuary Thou alone canst enter. Living thus with God, penetrating the mysteries of infinite charity, our contemplation should merge into adoration, and our life become transformed beneath this blessed light which shows us God so close to us—in us. Here in this interior heaven, I wish to recollect myself at each *Gloria Patri* which we repeat so often in the course of the day; at every hymn which terminates in praise of Thy glory—in the manifold occasions which speak of Thee to the soul which is attentive and faithful. Here, I shall adore Thee during the Holy Sacrifice of the Mass, which renews for us each day the immolation of Calvary, in the name of the Father and of the Son and of the Holy Ghost. Here also will my Whole religious life be spent—my life of union and of recollection, wherein I shall hear the voice of the Holy Spirit inviting me to those mysterious graces and divine realities which Thou dost so long to communicate to the children of Carmel. Who shall speak of those marvels of grace, those depths of love, which Thou dost reserve here, *ab intus* for the soul that knows how to wait for Thee and to listen for Thy voice?

Under the guidance of St Teresa, let us penetrate into these hidden mansions of the heavenly 'Interior Castle', even into the bridal-chamber, where in silence and tranquillity, 'recollected within myself', I shall in truth adore Thee, Oh my God, for 'they who are able to enclose themselves within this little heaven of the soul.... will come without fail to drink of the water of the fountain of life'.[3]

'There Thou wilt show me
That which my soul desired'.[4]

　　Thou wilt inundate me, as with a river of peace: *Ecce ego declinavi super eam quasi fluvium pacis*'.[5]

'Oh Trinity, Thou Who art prisoner of my love'![6]

[3] St Teresa: *Way of Perfection*, Ch. XXVIII.
[4] St John of the Cross: *Spiritual Canticle*, St. 38.
[5] Isaias 66, 12.
[6] St Thérèse of the Child Jesus: *Poems*.

HELP ME TO FORGET MYSELF UTTERLY....*

> *I was brought to nothing and I knew not;* [7]
> 'To love is to forget oneself,
> To lose oneself in the Beloved,
> Within the burning furnace of His Love.
> The true lover lives no longer in himself
> But feels the need of ceaseless self-oblivion'. [8]

Oh my God, Trinity Whom I adore, help me to forget myself completely....

To forget oneself—forget oneself completely, is not this the perfection of the *abneget semetipsum*!

To forget oneself: this is, as it were, the last degree of renunciation. To renounce self implies still some sort of return upon self,

*Grounding her ideas on the dogma of the Divine Indwelling, has not St Thérèse dared to formulate the following petition in her Act of Oblation to Merciful Love: 'Dwell in me as Thou dost in the Tabernacle —never abandon Thy little victim'. Some writers have asserted that the little Saint shewed by this time that she desired the real and permanent presence of the Sacred Species in her soul, and that her prayer was granted. No one can be certain of this, but it proves what importance she attached to the practice of having unceasing recourse to God within her, and to the ceaseless adoration of the Blessed Trinity in her pure soul—And this is the oft-recurring theme of many of her poems:

> 'Thy sanctuary here, dear Lord, am I,
> That evil men shall never dare molest;
> Rest in my heart! Oh do not pass me by!
> Thy garden I, each flower an offering blest'.
> (Remember Thou)

> 'My heaven is God alone, the Trinity Divine,
> Who dwells within my heart, the Prisoner of my love.
> There, contemplating Thee, I tell Thee Thou art mine;
> Thee will I love and serve until we meet above'.
> (My Heaven on Earth)

> 'To live of love, 'tis in my heart to guard
> A mighty treasure in a fragile vase'.
> (To Live of Love)

[7] *Canticle of Canticles.*
[8] *Poems of Sister Elizabeth.*

36

a victory, even, of the will aided by grace—achieved not without the compensation of a sense of satisfaction if not of vain glory.

But self-forgetfulness is a more complete annihilation—perhaps the most humiliating form of detachment. Through self-forgetfulness one casts aside—as not worth considering—everything that might delay our progress. For the soul which is by nature egoistic is not forgetfulness of self the thing which seems most difficult—most opposed to our natural tendencies? For it means the putting-aside of oneself, trampling on self-love, the death of the 'ego' always so assertive and so powerful.

Self-forgetfulness—this is the proof of a love which is pure, disinterested, perfect; which goes beyond the precept, and wants to love its neighbour *more* than itself, seeing in him the image of the God Whom it adores.

It is to make a void within oneself—to tend resolutely to nakedness of spirit, indispensable for the life of union, 'to go out from self, lose sight of self, to forsake self—in order to enter more deeply into Him at every instant. It is, moreover, to love God above all. A soul which has concentrated all its powers of loving in God alone—and whom God has introduced into His love, can no longer stop at those petty preoccupations which held her a captive to created things and to herself. She beholds everything from this profound centre, and encloses these things of earth within the eternal angle, which is determined solely by the good-pleasure of God.

'When the soul is so deeply fixed in Him as to be rooted in Him, the divine sap flows freely through it, and destroys whatever in its life was trivial, imperfect, and unspiritual. Thus stripped of self, and clothed with Jesus Christ, it has nothing to fear from without or within: all such things, far from being an obstacle, only root it more deeply in the love of its Master'.[9]

It is rare indeed to find a soul which is truly self-forgetful to such a point as this; for it supposes a corresponding degree of detachment and simplicity of heart. Even in the contemplative life, prolonged solitude and habitual reflection seem often to foster the tendency most opposed to this blessed self-oblivion.

[9] Last Retreat, 13th Day.

Certain souls will always tend to fall back on self, losing precious time in endless introspection—exaggerating the least difficulty or temptation, pitying themselves in their little trials; far from forgetting themselves they develop an over-refined sensitiveness which is touched and wounded by everything: others will seek themselves in spiritual direction, and even during prayer in consolations, sweetnesses and sensible delights.

Our holy Father St John of the Cross has written in detail of the various purifications through which spiritual persons must necessarily pass in order to come to that blessed state of forget-fulness of all created things—without which Divine Union cannot be attained, for 'God cannot possess a heart which is not free'. On the contrary, the more the soul enters into an absolute solitude and withdrawal, and 'the sooner it reaches this restful tranquillity, the more abundantly does it become infused with the spirit of Divine wisdom which is the loving, tranquil, lonely, peaceful, sweet inebriator of the spirit. Hereby the soul feels itself to be gently and tenderly wounded and ravished, knowing not by whom, nor whence, nor how'. [10]

Oh my God, help me to forget myself utterly!.. A Carmelite who lives this prayer, is surely already on the sure road to holiness. Help me, oh my God, to become such a soul—always and utterly self-regardless. Then shall I be truly humble, sub-missive, docile, devoted, serviceable, faithful, charitable, mortified, apostolic.

I shall become an instrument vibrating beneath the touch of grace; I shall be in the hands of my Heavenly Father, the grain of mustard-seed which He buries in good soil; dying daily in order to give birth, amidst the darkness, to the future harvest.

Then I shall launch forth in full sail boldly—without recoil, without groping, like a soul which is truly free, which neither petty returns on self nor personal considerations can hold back. I shall be utterly happy, because the eye of my soul will be fixed on God and on Eternity. Disregarding myself completely, I shall fly towards Him, I shall dwell in Him, and 'He will satisfy all

[10]St John of the Cross: *Living Flame*, Stanza III, 38.

my powers of loving. He will then have taken possession of every faculty and filled every void'.[11]

Little St Thérèse has left us this precious testimony: 'I found happiness on the day whereon I began to forget self.'[12] And Sister Elizabeth of the Trinity, developing this thought which was so dear to her, writes : 'I think the secret of peace and happiness lies in self-forgetfulness, in not being pre-occupied with self—which does not mean that we shall not feel our physical and moral ills.... God would have you go out from yourself, leaving aside every pre-occupation in order to retire into that solitude which He has chosen for Himself in the depths of your heart.... It may seem difficult to you to forget self.... don't think of yourself at all—if you only knew how simple this is! I will tell you my secret: think of God Who dwells within you, Whose temple you are. It is St Paul who tells us this, and we can believe him. Gradually the soul becomes accustomed to live in His blessed company. She understands that she bears within herself a little heaven wherein the God of love has fixed His dwelling; she then breathes as it were a divine atmosphere; I would even say that her body alone remains on earth, for her soul dwells beyond the veil in Him Who is unchangeable'.[13]

'It seems to me that the saints are people who forget themselves on every occasion—losing themselves in Him they love—with no returns upon self, no stopping at creatures—so that they can say with St Paul: "It is no longer I that live; it is Jesus Christ Who lives in me". To arrive at this transformation, one must of course immolate oneself—but we love sacrifice because we love our Crucified Saviour. Oh! look well at Him, offer Him your soul—tell Him you want to love Him alone. He will do everything for us, seeing that by ourselves we are too weak; and it is so good to be the little child of the good God'.[14]

[11]Souvenirs.
[12]St Thérèse: *Autobiography*.
[13]Souvenirs.
[14]*Ibid*.

SO THAT I MAY ESTABLISH MYSELF IN THEE, CHANGELESS AND CALM

It is necessary that your whole soul with all its faculties and all its powers, should be recollected in God and make but one spirit with Him.

St Albert the Great. *Union with God*—Chap. V.

OH my God, Trinity Whom I adore, help me to become utterly forgetful of self, so that I may establish myself in Thee—changeless and calm.

The goal of self-forgetfulness is then God's taking possession of the soul, of our whole being, bringing it to such a state of stability and passivity that it will be really established in God—changeless and calm.

This is union, the state of union—a very elevated degree of the spiritual life, to which all other stages converge. It is the summit to which every Carmelite soul should tend, under the influence of grace.

Prayers, silence, solitude, voluntary detachment from all around us—these have no other object than to dispose the soul for divine union. Prayer teaches us to find God and to dwell in Him. Silence, to hear the voice of the Beloved, to lead the faculties to recollection, to interior silence without which they would be an obstacle to the free unfolding of the life of grace. The rôle of the eremitical side of Carmelite life is to help us to find the Creator in solitude and the absence of creatures; the Creator Who alone can fill our heart and soul.

Non in commotione Dominus; The Lord is not to be found in agitation. How often have we experienced the truth in this in Carmel, more than elsewhere! If our spirit is dissipated, our nature in turmoil, our heart agitated, the Lord cannot repose there—for He is the Peaceful One.

In accordance with our daily life, our prayer, which is in some sort the expansion of our interior life, tends essentially to reflect this double character of peace and stability; *Inquire pacem et persequere eam*—'Follow after peace and pursue it'. Note well, that our Holy Rule never employs the term 'meditation' as do so many others; it speaks of *prayer*. Prayer means communing with God, heart to heart—the repose of the soul in God, intimacy of faith and of love—of love in faith, and of faith through love.

How shall we be able to pray in truth if the soul is not established in God, in peace? For the least thing that troubles it —be it ever so small—prevents it, at the outset, from being attentive to the divine whisper—in silence and recollection.

Interior or exterior disturbance, ill-regulated zeal, a too-feverish activity, vehement desires, random thoughts excited by created things—all these are simply obstacles, usurping in us the place which God alone should hold.

We know this so well, even though we may possess in only a slight degree the habit of recollection and fidelity to grace. The soul is not 'about its Father's business', [15] since it feels it is not free and at peace. Oh my God! help me to establish myself in Thee, changeless and calm!.... [16]

This means that Thy love must over-rule everything in me, that it must possess me utterly, so that I may become estranged from all things earthly, that my heart may be attached to nothing, and my soul, soaring above this world, may live with Thee— entirely in Heaven!

Entirely in Heaven, borne upwards by the wings of contemplation—there where the air is so pure, flooded with light, bathed in the supernatural.

Entirely in Heaven, in this *deep centre*, this little intimate heaven, wherein the Three Divine Persons hold unceasingly their counsels of love.

Entirely in Heaven, supported on the wings of the 'Divine Eagle', my gaze fixed on high and ever higher, amidst the

[15] St Luke II, 49.

[16] In the Venerable John of St Samson *Vray esprit de Carmel*, Chapter III we find these words: 'There (that is, in the sight and experimental knowledge of eternity) you will be made simple and changeless.... so that you can offer yourself to those 'deaths' which present themselves incessantly to the soul that desires to give proof of its fidelity to God— forcing it to turn to Him continually, and to dwell in Him in a fixed and total immutability, and to adhere to Him eternally'.

41

inebriating joy of this powerful flight towards the sun of Divine Love, where human things no longer have any place.

Oh my God, the more deeply Thou dost establish me in Thyself, the more will my supernatural horizon be enlarged. The more I recollect my powers—by the effort of my will aided by grace—in this profound intimacy, changeless and calm, the more wilt Thou tranquillize every discordant tendency which might prove an obstacle to the reign of the Immutable within my soul.

Whether I am in a state of consolation, aridity or weariness, it will make no difference to me. 'It is the law of this land of exile that we must pass through one state after another; I shall believe that Thou never changest, and that in Thy goodness Thou art always bending over me'—ready to bear me away and establish me in Thyself, in that solitude into which Thou desirest to 'lead the soul in order to speak to her heart'[17] in an ineffable manner.

17Osee II, 14.

AS THOUGH MY SOUL WERE ALREADY IN ETERNITY[18]

Within the heaven of the soul, the Praise of Glory begins already her Office of eternity.

WHAT a stimulating thought for a Carmelite! To act always in the light of eternity. Within the angle of eternity.... To behold creatures through the eyes of God, to be superior to human contingencies, to pass over the nothings which detain so many souls in the region of the common-place and ephemeral.

Quid ad aeternitatem?.... If we ask ourselves that question often, and if honestly, each evening, we weigh our day in the balance of eternity, shall we not advance rapidly in the way of detachment, fidelity and union?

Quid ad aeternitatem?—If our imagination scours the country for a trifle which it fancies, if the spirit is filled with all the dissipating thoughts it gathers on the way; if the heart allows itself to be agitated like a stormy sea on account of some opposition offered to our petty plans and desires and customs .... are we then 'workers for eternity'?

But if, suddenly stopping short, we listen to that interior voice reminding us of eternity, all these miserable trifles which create the storm within us, will fade into insignificance, and we shall regret the time wasted by attaching any importance to them, and so often magnifying them. How heavy will our responsibility appear to us, and how deplorable our slackness in co-operating with the Divine action.

We easily exert great will-power for the accomplishing of some passing work, to attain some goal of human activity; but when there is question of carrying out the wish of Christ, 'Dwell in Me, and I in you',[19] in order to concentrate all our energies towards the sublime life of union, are we not lacking

[18]We find exactly the same thought expressed by St Albert the Great: 'Strive only to live alone with God, above the things of this world, in a kind of spiritualized life, *as though your soul were already in eternity*, and separated from your body'.

[19]St John XV, 4.

alas, in sustained effort? If we let ourselves be distracted, pre-occupied, or dissipated, our interior life will escape miserably through the many cracks in the too-fragile vase of our recollection.

Help me, oh my God, to establish myself in Thee, as though my soul were already in eternity....

Eternity—what is it but heaven, happiness without limit, immortal beatitude, the possession of Thee, oh my God, the consummation of the union of love begun here below in the obscurity of faith.

Eternity—again what is it but the final goal of our earthly existence, for we are created only that we might be for God a praise of glory eternally. Our Carmelite vocation, more than any other, is directed to this end, in view of which we wish to suffer, to make reparation, to expiate, and to love. What would we not do, in order that in eternity there might be one more soul to glorify God?—that our soul, by its growth in grace, might render Him a greater glory for all eternity? The more we disengage ourselves from things of earth, the more will our eyes be fixed instinctively on eternity. Gradually, it will become impossible to distract their attention.

Also, it is indeed only from above, that the soul which is established in God views all things, in peace and tranquillity, without effort, without shadow, disengaged from every human consideration which would render it more or less subservient to the senses and passions.

To establish myself in Thee, as though my soul were already in eternity—all proportion guarded, this is *to live always in the heaven of my soul*, in union with the Father, the Son and the Holy Spirit; it is to expect all from Thee, to attribute all to Thee, giving Thee full liberty to act in me and through me, Oh Adorable Trinity.

It is said that at the moment of death the eye of the soul is illumined and beholds everything in the light of eternity. And grace is given to it whereby it understands through the eyes of God. Let us ask this grace even now; it will not be refused to us.[20] Let us take our stand, without fear, on the threshold of eternity and we shall be astonished to see things so clearly!

'For in the light of eternity, the soul beholds all things in their true centre. Then, how fruitless will seem everything that has not been done for God and with God.... Mark everything with the seal of love, it alone will endure for ever'.[21]

'At eventide they will examine thee in love'.[22] Upon *effective* love, love which has proved itself by deeds, love which will have amassed wealth for eternity, not recoiling before effort and sacrifice, but responding fully to the divine expectation.

Oh, that this judgment might be for Carmelites truly one of love. Would that love would make of our lives a burning fire in which all our faults and imperfections might be consumed. May Love be able to plead for us through the voice of countless souls saved through our immolation, who will welcome us with the Lamb without spot among the 'Blessed of His Father'.[23]

[20]For the soul which lives in intimate union with God present within it, this grace is accompanied by the infused gifts of the Holy Ghost. Is not this the underlying motive of its seeming indifference to the things of earth, its detachment, and habitual disposition of *Sursum Corda?* Such a soul no longer needs to make any effort to revert to this thought and to draw from it a practical conclusion wherewith to stimulate its life. By its union with God, it lives so to speak in an anticipated eternity.

St Thérèse of the Child Jesus, and Sister Elizabeth of the Trinity both give abundant proof of this throughout their writings, which are filled with the fragrance of eternity diffused by their contemplative souls. This interior gaze towards the immortal had become natural to them, because God dwelt in them and possessed them completely.

[21]Souvenirs.
[22]St John of the Cross: *Spiritual Sentences and Maxims*, 57.
[23]St Matthew XXV, 34.

MAY NOTHING DISTURB MY PEACE, NOR DRAW ME FORTH FROM THEE, OH MY IMMUTABLE LORD....

Let nothing trouble thee, nothing disturb thee,
God alone suffices.

(St Teresa's Bookmark)

IN order to maintain a steady ascent towards divine union, it is absolutely necessary to have one's soul established in peace. No one, of course, will arrive at this summit except by gradual progress, for the obstacles to interior peace are innumerable. We carry them within us, in our nature, our character, our education, our hereditary defects, in our mind and in our heart. We find them outside ourselves, in the wear-and-tear of common life, in the trials God sends us, and all the little providential happenings which are destined to strengthen us in virtue. We find them in a more hidden though not less certain form in the temptations permitted by God, in the cunning and constant attacks of the evil one, who desires nothing so much as to rob us of our peace, for he knows well—this prince of darkness, how a disturbed soul is at once deprived of supernatural light. And if one is not on one's guard, it seems that—in the case of certain religious—a mere nothing suffices to darken the spirit and throw it into disorder. Superficial souls these—not stabilised in love and in the art of giving. Such a soul, thinking it has complete mastery of itself, will end by tormenting itself and losing its recollection at the least wisp of straw which lies in its path.

The result of physical fatigue, or nervous exhaustion.... the moral effect of solitude and of introspection.... the spiritual effect of purifications which are necessary for placing the soul in a state of humility and keeping it therein.... it matters not. The soul must re-act, and set about establishing itself in peace—above all it must *pray*. For the more a soul allows itself to be led by its impressions, the more it will be ruled by nature. This will lead it sometimes to great activity, sometimes to laziness; now to pride, under its many subtle and concealed forms, now to discouragement and immortification; always to relaxation and trouble.

Then will result the reign of caprice, of self-love, of self-will; the tedious succession of hours and days wherein the soul drags itself along discontented with itself and everything else because it is vegetating in a quagmire, and is not fulfilling its mission on this earth. It is like the dead branch, which would be better cut off since it yields no fruit.... it is the tepid water which Our Lord will vomit out of His mouth.

'Let not your heart be troubled.... my peace I leave unto you, my peace I give you; not as the world giveth do I give unto you.... I have overcome the world'.[24] *Non turbetur cor vestrum....* May nothing trouble my peace, oh my Immutable Lord, nor draw me forth from Thee—from the impregnable fortress of holy recollection'.

Nothing! neither trials, great or small, nor creatures, nor the devil, nor myself. My interior peace is the work of grace, it is true; but it is also the reward Thou wilt bestow on my efforts, on the generous struggle I shall have sustained in order to conquer-one-by-one, all the obstacles which lie in the way leading to divine tranquillity.

This peace is nothing but life in Thee, oh my Immutable Lord, life deeply enclosed within the mystery of the Indwelling of the Blessed Trinity in my soul. The more I live within, the more deeply shall I be rooted in peace. For, as grace takes possession of me more and more, it will soon prevent me from 'wandering from Thee'—except perhaps momentarily and only in order to make me seek again my true centre, that interior sanctuary which is my home and my life.

'And in order that nothing may draw me forth from this beautiful interior silence, I must keep myself always in the same condition, the same isolation, the same retirement, the same detachment. If my desires, my fears, my joys, or my sorrows, if all the impulses coming from these four passions are not completely subjected to God, I shall not be solitary: there will be

[24] St John XIV, 1, 27; XVI, 33.

47

turmoil within me. Therefore calm, the slumber of the powers the unity of the whole being are needed.'[25]

Oh perfect unity of my God! Oh my Immutable One.... make me even now while on earth to participate in Thy divine attributes of unity and immutability: may there be balance, equanimity in my interior and exterior life, in my spirit, in my soul. Unity in my acts—not allowing my forces to be scattered in secondary and divergent aims—often futile—but concentrated entirely in the unity of the divine Centre.

Oh my Immutable One!.... on this earth everything is passing, nothing is stable except Thee. Everything is marked with decay. And we know well this deficiency, because our soul is not made for passing things. Every separation wounds it and makes it suffer, every death creates in it a void which only the hope of eternity can heal, and every break tears it. Yes—the soul has need of that which endures, the heart must anchor itself in the unchangeable.

In Carmel especially, to accomplish our life-work, we must fasten on the true, the immortal. Detaching itself from terrestial things, the soul seeks the infinite. And our apostolic ideal would be a vain dream, if, grafted as we are upon the True Vine, our activity did not flow from this hidden and fruitful creative Immutability.

Our interior life even more, would be unstable and subject to illusion, if we did not centre it in the unity of a ruling power; if we did not ground it in love by means of suffering, in absolute truth, whole-heartedly, without wavering, without half-measures, without vacillations of the active or passive will.

If there are few stabilized souls, it is because there are few who look only at the unique goal, the summit to be attained, directly, disencumbered of all superfluous goods, aware of what God expects of them, and firmly resolved (not with that enthusiasm which quickly passes, but with a strong and determined will)—not to stop, by the wayside; but to embrace the cross under all its forms; knowing that it is a liberating instrument which renders them free to respond fully and totally to the call of Christ.

[25]Last Retreat, 10th Day.

BUT MAY I PENETRATE MORE DEEPLY EVERY MOMENT INTO THE DEPTHS OF THY MYSTERY

How precious are these hours of our earthly pilgrimage, for on them alone depends our eternity. Each moment can be made the occasion of a more intense act of love, principle of a closer union with God, of a more powerful reflection of the beauty of God in our souls. And these moments are numbered.... Oh! the value of time!

(Cardinal Mercier)

WHAT is this 'mystery' if not the great mystery of love.... the Trinity in Unity, Unity in Trinity. This indeed was the whole mystery for the privileged soul of Sister Elizabeth of the Trinity.[26]

For other Carmelites, this mystery might have less spiritual significance. It is for each one to follow in her interior life the special leading of the Holy Spirit, Who destines one soul for the more special contemplation of this mystery, others for another. It was thus that God revealed to St Thérèse of the Child Jesus the secrets hidden in His Adorable Face and in the way of spiritual childhood. And it is the peculiar merit of this little Sister to have understood them under divine illumination, to have penetrated them by a perfect correspondence with grace, and to have adapted them to her spiritual life.

In Carmel, many souls strive to reproduce the hidden life of Nazareth. Others will be captivated by the Blessed Virgin, and will follow the pure footsteps of Mary, Queen and Beauty of Carmel, so that she may lead them to intimacy with the Word.

To others again, the divine Master reveals in a new light some mystery of His Passion. Our holy Mother St Teresa lived for a

[26] Or rather, may it not be that of the Incarnate Word, this mystery of love 'which was manifested in the flesh, was justified in the spirit, appeared unto angels, hath been preached unto the Gentiles, is believed in the world, is taken up into glory'. (I Tim. III, 16), the eternal mystery of our love, for 'to me to live is Christ' (Phil.I, 21). The life of Mother Mary of Jesus, Foundress of the Carmel of Paray-le-Monial, would lead one to suppose this.

long time on the interior vision of the *Ecce Homo*, or on the consideration of the Agony, and declares that it is the sacred Humanity of our Saviour which must lead us to the Trinity. Our holy Father St John of the Cross affirms: 'for progress comes not save through the imitation of Christ, Who is the Way, the Truth, and the Life, and no man comes to the Father but by Him.... Elsewhere He says: "I am the door; by Me if any man enter in he shall be saved".'[27] 'Two things serve the soul as wings whereby it is able to rise to union with God: these are affective compassion for the death of Christ and for our neighbour.'[28]

For compassionate souls, the Passion is, without doubt, the Mystery *par excellence* which moves and stimulates them, causing them to share in the great work of redemption. The cross will ever lead to heroism and sanctity. It must of necessity have its place in every perfect life. To conceal its preponderating rôle would lead to illusion.

Who can justly appreciate the value of these attractions of grace, and affirm that one mystery is superior to another, with regard to the practical result derived from the contemplation thereof? The essential point is, that by the contemplation of the mystery, the soul should become convinced of the necessity of suffering and the cross,[29] should practise self-renunciation and dispose itself for Divine Union.

[27]St John of the Cross: *Sentences*.

[28]St John of the Cross: *Spiritual Sayings* No. 7.

[29]Rev. Fr Pascal du Saint-Sacrement: (Introduction to *The Entrance into Divine Wisdom*) The most infallible proof and one most worthy of acceptance, of the action of grace in a soul, is a tendency to mortification. Love of the cross is the undeniable evidence of divine love. The authentic touch of the Holy Spirit—more especially when it inundates the soul with consolations, imparts an experimental knowledge of the obstacles which the soul opposes to perfect union, whence results, in the case of genuine saints, an imperative need of waging a deadly war against themselves even to their last breath. Did not St John of the Cross crucify the flesh by bodily suffering, and the soul even to the point of consenting to total despoliation? This alone is the safe way.

What a vain subterfuge it is then, what a lamentable error, and

Then, there is reason to hope that it will not take a false road, and that it will allow itself to be guided in truth by the Spirit of God—He Who ever remains sovereign Master in every work of sanctity, and 'the principal agent'.[30] Now this Spirit, essentially free, breathes where He wills and as He wills.

But if the mystery of the Most Holy Trinity surpasses others in excellence, there is every evidence that, without a special grace of illumination, this mystery still remains for many souls, alas! the most impenetrable and the most inert as to the influence it exercises on their efforts towards perfection.

Let us allow ourselves then to be led on the wings of grace according to the impulse of the Holy Spirit; He will reveal to us the special mystery which will lead us more deeply into God, so that we may live in a continual union of faith, which of necessity carries with it our growth in love.

Each moment should see in us the surging of this double current: each moment should be, in Carmel, a moment of eternity. Do we really believe this?

How many lost moments there are in our daily life! Moments of infidelity, of un-watchfulness, of negligence, of levity.... moments of greater faults, useless or culpable talkativeness, loss of time over our duties, voluntary returns on self, laziness, susceptibility, pride, little self-seekings in everything and through everything!....

How many moments when even in choir, at prayer, Divine Office, before the Most Blessed Sacrament, our dissipated soul and spirit—empty or lazy—do not co-operate at all with the divine action which is ever ready to expand in us—but put obstacles in its way, and impede by a deceptive inconsistency the growth of grace.

dangerous deception, to make little of the cross and allow souls to slumber in a sweet quietude—hiding the difficulties from them.

.... Let upright souls be on their guard against false interpretations of the pure teaching of the Gospel, as the great mystical Doctor of Carmel warns us: 'every spirit which pretends to advance along a sweet and easy path, but fears to imitate Christ, does not seem to me good'.

[30] St John of the Cross: *Living Flame* St. III 29.

Oh! these lost moments—lost for ever in that past which each minute lengthens, as it passes lightly by, devoid of good, useless for God's glory—and of no merit alas! for our poor soul in the eyes of God!....

Oh! these lost moments!.... what a dead weight they will be in the balance for many religious if they are not on their guard. May they not, in the long run, be the reason why many a soul leads a commonplace and ineffectual existence even on this summit of Carmel where we ought to be on fire with zeal and love. What deplorable inconsistency can they create in consecrated souls, who ought to be entirely given up to love but often remain below the standard of many others, in spite of all the spiritual helps drawing them towards the heights and surrounding them with the radiance of the ideal.

Moments lost!—while sinners await them, priests need them, while the Church counts on their power of intercession and reparation, and our dear Saviour, from His Cross, sorrowfully calls us to order!

The depth of Thy mystery, oh my God, is the abyss of love. Draw my soul more and more into this profound centre wherein Thou dwellest, and which is illumined by Thy radiance. May I learn therein not to squander these brief moments of my earthly existence, precious moments of my life as a Carmelite, but may each one lead me further into the knowledge of Thy goodness and to the plenitude of union.

May I learn there also the the sublime science of love— science which no wordly *savant* can penetrate as deeply as the humble and unlettered, enlightened by the Divine Spirit, 'because Thou hast hidden these things from the wise and prudent and hast revealed them to little ones, oh my God'.[31]

'Who then shall separate me from the love of Jesus Christ? Shall tribulation—or distress, or famine, or nakedness or danger or persecution, or the sword? As it is written: For Thy sake we are put to death all the day long: we are accounted as sheep for the slaughter. But in all these things we overcome, because of Him that hath loved us. For I am sure that neither death, nor life,

[31] St Luke X, 21.

nor angels, nor principalities, nor powers, nor things present, nor things to come, nor might, nor height, nor depth, nor any other creature, shall be able to separate us from the love of God which is in Christ Jesus Our Lord'.[32]

[32]Romans VIII, 35-39.

GIVE PEACE TO MY SOUL

Domine Deus, pacem da nobis, omnia enim praestitisti nobis, pacem quietis, pacem Sabbathi, pacem sine vespera.

(St Augustine. Conf.)

THERE are few souls who are truly at peace, even in religious life, because few are truly mortified and supernatural. And, as union cannot take place except in peace, God will not enter with His gifts into a heart that is not void, tranquil and pacified.

This true peace cannot be obtained without, on the one hand, self-denial, filial abandonment, and prayer—and on the other by purifying trials and grace: grace especially, for this is a matter for two—the work of the soul and the work of God. The soul must will sincerely, must set to work energetically to remove those personal obstacles for which it is responsible, and which impede the expansion of divine peace within it. In contemplative orders, both the common and the eremitical life provide a vast field.

It may happen that the jarring of characters, temperaments, or even of spiritual aims, will become pre-occupations for the spirit, and be injurious to interior peace, if one does not adopt at the outset an attitude of unshaken determination not to stop at these things.

Without this constant practice of nakedness of spirit, so necessary for the soul's progress, these preoccupations will gradually people its solitude with everything that the senses may have registered in passing, and its interior heaven will soon be nothing more than a miserable kaleidoscope, composed of a motley collection of morbid imaginations, the love of God being the only absent factor. Where ideas and fancies chase each other like this, the result cannot but be trouble, disquiet, and lack of peace.

Our interior peace may also be put to the test by a purifying trial sent by God. In the development of every spiritual life there occur moments of temptation, searching trials, profound darkness, wherein the soul struggles painfully in the mystery of the invisible, in those dark nights which our Father St John of the Cross has described so minutely.

When the soul has fought the good fight, God, when He so wills, will begin to establish it in the knowledge of its wretchedness, and to grant it the gift of peace.

Pax!.... Peace—is not this the atmosphere most favourable to the unfolding of the contemplative life—the translucent atmosphere, wherein the flowers of the cloister bloom, wherein privileged souls live and die—souls which God keeps for Himself alone in the enclosed garden?

Can one imagine a monastery anything but an oasis of peace? Its high walls seem to guard it against the turmoil and agitation of this feverish age in which we live; its very approach breathes peace, of which silence and solitude are the watchful custodians.

What an attraction for souls enamoured of an ideal! How many have experienced the captivating charm of this divine peace, invading them at times like the hidden radiance of the Presence of Jesus!

Although these externals are but the outward expression of the peace within, they are nevertheless, necessary for the development of interior peace, and are of more importance than some restless people would believe. But the *essential thing, however, is interior peace, the calming of our interior dwelling so that God may become its abiding and ruling Guest.*

'Keep your soul in this state of calm and tranquillity for the love of God; you will then find your Master not only near you but *in you*.... and you will become convinced of this truth, that the Divine Will ever desires our happiness', said P. de Bonilla to the religious of his day, in his precious little Treatise on peace of soul. [33]

The lesson is ever the same: souls do not change. *To arrive at union with God, the soul must be established in peace.* To attain this state of tranquillity, we have only to understand the gift of God, which strips, purifies, purges, according to the degree of union to which He intends to raise the soul, and to the soul's faithfulness and strength.

[33] *Treatise on Peace of Soul*: translated by P. Ubald d'Alencon.

And 'while the soul simplifies and ennobles itself, while the joy of its freedom makes it exult, a feeling of balance takes possession of its innermost being. It feels that everything within it, impressions, ideas, resolutions, actions, range themselves in order: and from the contemplation of this order.... springs the pacification of its whole moral being: "Much peace have they that love Thy Law, Oh God!" ' (Ps. C. XVIII)[34]

Give peace to my soul, oh my God! I know how much Thy grace must aid me in this ascent towards Thee, for of myself I can do nothing; and repeatedly, through a disconcerting cowardice, I expose myself to the assaults of the devil who longs at all costs to disturb me.

Give peace to my soul, oh my God! And the 'Word will rise up from that peace wherein He dwells with the Father and the Holy Spirit, and will overshadow this soul, and she will behold all things in God'. She will be able to realise Thy eternal designs, to unite herself intimately to Thee in love and faith, and to render Thee that glory to which Thou hast called and predestined her. 'For where is true peace and glory to be found? Is it not in Me? *Ubi est pax et vera gloria?.... Nonne in me?*'[35]

[34]*Ibid.*
[35]*Imitation of Christ* Bk. III Ch. 28.

MAKE IT THY HEAVEN, THY CHERISHED DWELLING PLACE, THE PLACE OF THY REPOSE

Heaven is not the only dwelling-place of Our Lord; He has another in the soul, which may be called another heaven.

(Saint Teresa)

To what a sublime vocation Thou hast called me, oh my God! To be Thy heaven, Thy chosen dwelling-place, the place of Thy repose! 'To say that we bear heaven within us!....' Before such a mystery of grace and love I can only annihilate myself in adoration and thanksgiving.

It is then quite lawful for us to live by anticipation in the happiness of heaven, to possess heaven within us, *to find there unceasingly—'by a movement wholly simple and loving, the Divine Guest of our soul'.*[36]

Portando Deum caeli, caelum sumus'.[37] Bearing within us the God of heaven, we ourselves are heaven. This phrase is the logical expression of the thought of Sister Elizabeth of the Trinity: 'I have found heaven already, because heaven is God, and God is in my soul'.

This is the teaching of Christ Himself—the doctrine of the Church set forth by St Paul, developed by the Fathers, commented by the doctors, practised all down the ages by a multitude of saints and pious souls. *When we possess sanctifying grace, God is present in us, and we are 'Christ-bearers', Christopheri*! thus has St Ignatius of Antioch eulogised it.

Living faith in this mystery of God dwelling in us by sanctifying grace, is, as it were, the basis of the work of our sanctification.[38]

[36]Souvenirs.

[37]St Augustine. In Psalm LXXXVIII.

[38]The Indwelling of the Blessed Trinity in our soul, the centre whence our entire spiritual life is derived, and to which it returns, is guaranteed to us by theology (*L'Amour de Dieu et la Croix de Jesus* pp. 659-60-61. Garrigou-Lagrange, O.P.) It shows us first of all, what is this special presence in the souls of the just who have arrived at the full and fixed development of the life of grace—that is to say in the souls of the Blessed in heaven. It is certain, according to divine revelation, that in heaven the

57

Caelum es, et in caelum ibis.[39] Heaven thou art, and to Heaven shalt thou go!

Heaven—the beatific vision—truly this is the longed-for goal of our pilgrimage—the end of all our aspirations.

Heaven! Is it not eternal life, pure love, the possession of all that faith and hope promise us from the Infinite Good that is God, Unity in Trinity.

soul of each one of the Blessed is a living spiritual tabernacle wherein the Blessed Trinity, really present, is known as It knows Itself, loved and eternally glorified. In each beatified soul, the fullness of grace, which is a participation in the divine nature, is the principle whence derives the light of glory, which causes it to see immediately the divine essence, in a far better way than we ever 'see' here below, the persons with whom we speak, because these persons are exterior to us: while the Blessed Trinity seen unveiled is most intimate to the beatified soul, which it maintains in existence and in the divine life.

Now the life of grace and of charity, is, here and now, radically the same as that of heaven. 'If thou didst know the gift of God', said the Saviour to the Samaritan woman, 'thou wouldst have asked me to give thee to drink.... and I would have given Thee living water, springing up into life everlasting'. The life of grace is eternal life already begun, for when sanctifying grace which is in us, shall have attained its full development, and shall have been confirmed so as to be no longer capable of being lost, it will become glory, and will be the fundamental principle of the beatific vision: as for the love which is in our heart, it will remain eternally. There are, doubtless, two essential differences between the life of a christian on earth and in heaven; here, in this world, we can only know God in the obscurity of faith, and we can lose Him; whereas in heaven, we shall know Him in the clarity of vision, and shall possess Him without any possibility of losing Him. But in spite of these two differences the life is fundamentally the same; grace is the seed of glory— *semen gloriae*—just as the life which is latent in the acorn is the same as in the fully-developed oak, and the rational life which is dormant in the child is the same as that which appears in the full-grown man. To sum up: 'In the soul of each one of the just, the *special* presence of God, Author of all grace, is at once *real, objective, and effective*; it is the presence of an object, not at a distance, but *really present in us*, and so to speak, known experimentally', says St Thomas (*Cf.* Ia dist. 14q2 a.2 ad 3).

[39]Origen.

Heaven! It is the glory of God, the multitude of the blessed eternally prostrating in adoration before the throne of the Lamb! And in order that there may be an ever greater number of souls to sing for all eternity the 'new canticle'—thus adding to the grandeur of this scene, we Carmelites desire to co-operate in the work of redemption.

To be able to commence, even now, in the heaven of our souls this office of eternity—is not this one of the most consoling truths of faith?

If only we thought more about it!—Generally speaking, it is not faith which is lacking, but the works of faith.

We believe the testimony of the Word, the basis of this doctrine: 'If anyone will love me, My Father will love him, and we will come and make our abode with him'. We know that Jesus several times repeated this same teaching during His sacerdotal prayer, from which we should conclude how important is this His supreme counsel.

Alas! we do not make it the object of sustained and supreme effort in our spiritual life.

What a prospect however, to be a tabernacle, to be heaven! Behold the sublime ideal which will become a reality for the soul which lives in a state of grace!—I am heaven: does not this impose the obligation of striving to bring something of heaven into my life—always more of heaven. *To sow the seed of eternity in time.* Is there any other purpose of our earthly existence? Is there anyone who, after reflection, would wish to fix elsewhere the goal of his life?'[40]

Who would wish to remain insensible to the desire of the Heart of Christ, and to respond to it so half-heartedly, if he had heard from the lips of Jesus the words addressed to His Apostles; 'Abide in Me.... Abide in My Love'; with the accompanying promise, 'If you abide in Me you will bring forth much fruit'?

A soul which applies itself with faith, energy of will, and perseverance, to finding God present within it, at every moment of the day, penetrated by feelings of reverence and adoration in presence of the Divine Majesty, will become in a short time

[40]P. Plus, s.j.: *God Within Us.*

recollected, silent and fervent—always 'about its Father's business'.

For its 'conversation will be always in heaven', and the intimacy of love established between God and itself will be the prelude to its consummation in unity.

Unity! To live in unity, with the Father, the Son, and the Holy Spirit, does not this mean *to return at each moment to that inmost centre where God dwells*, and to wait upon Him there with such love that it may indeed be 'a cherished dwelling, a heaven, the place of His repose'.

'Let us take care that our house of God is completely possessed by the "Three"—This is the secret of holiness, and it is so simple'. [41]

Then, when God is truly present within us, He will fill us with Himself, He will inform all our acts, and inspire all our words.

The 'council' of the Three will be our guide in every difficulty, our light in every decision, the rule of all our directing. God will shine forth in us and through us; our works will become fruitful through the sap drawn from Him; *and we shall enjoy that promised union*; '*Ego in Te, et Tu in me*'.

Then will our hidden apostolate extend its influence, and then only shall we fulfill our obligations as Carmelites.

Make my soul, then, Thy heaven, oh my God, Thy cherished dwelling-place, the place of Thy repose.

With Sister Elizabeth I emphasise these words, '*cherished dwelling-place, and the place of Thy repose*'.

Thou dwellest, let us hope, in the soul of every religious. But could one say that it is always a *cherished* dwelling, and a place of *repose*?

When this heart and soul are occupied with self, dissipated by frivolous or disturbing thoughts—when this soul, which receives Thee each morning at the Holy Table leaves Thee alone all day, or during the greater part thereof, to grieve over her infidelities, her negligences, her tepidity, her backslidings....

When this soul, carried away by the duties of routine,

[41]Souvenirs.

recollects itself but little in order to prepare a dwelling less unworthy of Thee—

When it is filled with secondary interests, materialistic and trifling pre-occupations—

When it allows itself to be carried away by work or distractions of every kind—

When there is but little charity in the heart for one's neighbour and when the spirit is warped by pride under its many forms—
Oh my God! canst Thou make of such a soul a place of repose?

What comfort, what consolation couldst Thou find in such a one? It cannot compassionate Thy sufferings, for it is taken up with its own affairs and the things of earth.

I ask pardon, my God, for the miserable dwelling which many consecrated souls afford Thee.

Pardon, my God, for the poor dwelling I have so often given Thee.

Help me, so that henceforth my soul, unworthy of such great graces, may be for Thee always a heaven, a cherished dwelling, and oasis of sweet repose.

It will then respond to the ardent wish of Sister Elizabeth of the Trinity. 'Be the paradise of Jesus. He is so little known—so little loved! Open your heart wide so that He may enter it, and there, in your little interior cell, love Him. He thirsts for love; let us keep Him company'.[42]

[42] Ibid.

MAY I NEVER LEAVE THEE THERE ALONE, BUT KEEP ME THERE, ALL ABSORBED IN THEE, IN LIVING FAITH, ADORING THEE, AND WHOLLY YIELDED UP TO THY CREATIVE ACTION

A praise of Glory is a soul which contemplates God in faith and simplicity.

(Retreat, 10th Day)

'I have looked for hearts, and I have not found them'. This sorrowful complaint uttered by the Sacred Heart to St Margaret-Mary, might well be addressed to us, His privileged ones, His Carmelites, whenever we leave Him alone in our interior dwelling—alone in our insensible heart, instead of surrounding Him with loving attentions.

Solitude was the lot of Jesus during His sojourn on this earth. Solitude, isolation of His Divine Soul among creatures who could not understand Him. A relative solitude, however, for His spirit dwelt in fellowship of union with His Father and the Holy Spirit; and whenever He retired into solitude in order to pray, was it not in order to find Them more easily, and to be less alone on earth?

As for ourselves, few moral sufferings create so great a homesickness for Heaven as does this loneliness, in which one finds oneself, even—and more especially—in the midst of a crowd—but in a more painful way when surrounded by friends whose souls do not vibrate in unison with ours, and who do not see things from the same supernatural angle.

Jesus wished to taste this loneliness before us. He experiences it each day in the greater number of souls, and in so many of His consecrated ones.

It is generally through indifference, negligence, forgetfulness, that we leave God alone in us. But may we not see in these things a manifest proof of our dissipation of spirit—of our lack of love?

Oh, the solitude of God in our soul!—What a sad state of things for a daughter of the seraphic St Teresa! How many faults spring from it, how many religious lives are wasted because they turn aside from their aim.

For our spiritual transformation can only be brought about by union; and to leave God alone within us means that our efforts, our struggles, our resolutions, our strength for the ascent, will not derive their efficacy from this union.

To leave God alone in us is to misunderstand our Carmelite vocation, our call to the eremitical life gravitating around the Presence of God, source of light and fecundity.

The soul which is not occupied with God, which does not live by Him soon feels weighed down by solitude, and is overtaken by melancholy and discontent.

Then, if it is not faithful, it will seek for distraction, and open the door to every kind of relaxation and backsliding; for it no longer fulfills its mission on earth, it cannot obtain grace for other souls, since it has cut itself off from the source, and squandered the 'gift of God'.

Already Thou art left alone, oh my God, in so many tabernacles, where no one thinks of finding and adoring Thee. Thou art alone in so many Christians who communicate in the morning only to forget Thee during the rest of the day. Thou art alone in many a priestly heart, which is too much taken up with exterior works, not understanding the one thing necessary. And art Thou to remain alone also in the souls of Thy spouses?....

Oh my God, let it not be so. *We wish to live recollected in Thy Presence, to be there 'in adoration, wholly yielded up to Thy creative action'.*

Exterior recollection leads to interior recollection: it is the form, the safeguard of interior adoration.

Are not the most beautiful pictures of the Blessed Virgin those depicting her with head inclined, eyes lowered, wholly absorbed in deep contemplation of all 'those things which she kept in her heart'.[43]

Thus should the Carmelite ever be—a soul of prayer, of silence and of recollection, always on the alert for the voice of the Beloved; always 'watching in faith', as Sister Elizabeth expresses it. Yes, watching in faith, and not tepid or drowsy. Watching in faith—in order to ponder the great mysteries of which she is the

[43]St Luke, II 51.

63

recipient (often so ungrateful). In living faith, so as to live by faith, and more especially by this vigorous faith in God's indwelling in her. This mystery, if lived intensely, is so luminous: 'It is this intimacy with Him, living within me, which is the beautiful sun lighting my life, making it an anticipated heaven'.[44]

For then she will not be able to leave Him there alone: but she will become all adoration, wholly yielded up to His creative action. She will walk 'in innocence of heart in the midst of her house, always adoring God for His own sake, dwelling like Him in the eternal present in which He lives'.[45] 'For faith gives God even in this life—covered, it is true, with the veil in which He hides Himself—but God Himself nevertheless. "When that which is perfect is come (that is to say, the clear vision) then that which is imperfect (in other words, the knowledge given through faith) shall come to an end". Faith makes future blessings so certain and so present to us, that they are evolved in our soul and subsist there before we actually enjoy them. St John of the Cross tells us that faith serves as feet to take us to God, and that it is possession itself in an obscure manner. Faith alone can enlighten us concerning Him Whom we love, and we should choose it as the means of attaining divine union, for it fills the soul with all spiritual good things'.[46]

Is not the normal attitude of a Carmelite—(her own particular state, one might say) this adoration 'in spirit and in truth',[47] ceaseless adoration, which makes her commence while on earth, her eternal office of praise and thanksgiving? Is she not by her vocation, an *orante*, an adorer, a soul possessed by God, full of God, so that she is always giving God, for

'With His Virgin Mother, Christ has chosen her
    That at His Feet, by day and night, she might remain'.
'At His Feet', or amidst the tasks entrusted to her by obedience, adoration remains her principal duty—prayer by night and day, 'intimacy with God Who dwells in her, Who is more present to

44Souvenirs.
45Last Retreat, 10th Day.
46*Heaven on Earth* 8th Day.
47St John IV, 23.

her than she is to herself'.[48] By prayer, she yields herself up to the creative action of God—that entirely supernatural action which 'creates a new heart within her', and gives her soul a more and more perfect resemblance to the Father, the Son and the Holy Spirit.

For it is in prayer God opens up unfathomable depths which He fills according to their vast capacity.

There, He strips it of the old man, and re-clothes it in the new, which He transforms into Himself.

It is there His creative action supernaturalises unceasingly; disclosing and shedding light on unsuspected horizons where the soul is entirely renewed in spirit. There He heaps upon it the treasures of His Heart, and pours out His vivifying love which divinises, little by little, whatever it informs.

Cor mundum crea in me, Deus, et spiritum rectum innova in visceribus meis.[49]

It is truly a pure heart and an upright spirit which the work of grace creates in the docile soul; a pure heart which loves according to God, sees things from God's point of view, seeks only God; an upright spirit, no longer darkened by natural weakness, which does not evade the Divine Master's commands, which looks straight at the goal, above all obstacles, beyond the human ego with its defects and mediocrities.

Our whole spiritual life, and the progress of the soul, depends vitally on the creative action of God, which activates each effort, each elevation, each degree of progress in the way of perfection. It makes itself felt by its gifts and graces, by its inspirations and its pregnant silences. It effects the touch of love which lights up the road and renders the ascent easy. It disposes events pointing out in them the Divine Will to which we should adhere; it changes dispositions and tendencies, so that the soul may co-operate with the designs of eternal love.

The creative action of God—it is the breath of the Holy Spirit, *fons vivus, ignis, caritas*, this breath which will 'water our

[48]Souvenirs.
[49]Ps. L, 10.

dryness, bend our stubborn wills, warm our coldness, guide our wayward steps, transform all that it touches'.

'The mystic death becomes very simple and sweet to souls who yield themselves up to the divine action within the depths of their being. They think far less of the work of destruction and detachment left to them to accomplish than of plunging into the furnace of love burning within them—the same Love which in the Blessed Trinity is the bond between the Father and His Word. Such souls enter into Him by a living faith; there, in simplicity and peace, they are raised by Him above all things into the 'sacred darkness', and transformed into the divine image'.[50]

Oh my God, grant that I may surrender myself fully and without delay to Thy creative action, so that it may freely infuse into me the life-giving sap which will absorb all the impurities, all the dross, which impede the growth of the divine virtues in my soul.

Oh my God, may I yield myself up utterly to Thy creative action! It will make me holy, pure, less unworthy of possessing Thee, and relishing Thy presence within me.

[50]*Heaven on Earth* 6th Day.

OH MY CHRIST WHOM I ADORE! CRUCIFIED BY LOVE!

With Christ I am nailed to the Cross

(Gal. 11, 19)

OH my Christ Whom I adore! Let us recollect ourselves for a moment beneath the great scene of Calvary.

Christ, our adored Christ, is there, crushed by sorrow, dying of love for mankind. In that rending cry of His eternal *Sitio*, He saw my soul, He counted on my fulfilling the mission of coredemptrix.

He thirsted for souls, especially for consecrated souls who would spread His love—like an immense furnace even to the ends of the earth.

He thirsted to be loved by these souls, loved supremely, even to folly—even to martyrdom, even to the cross.

Then, beholding in the light of eternity the vast multitude of such souls, and stretching out His two bleeding Arms to invite them all to continue His work, He inclined His Head towards them, and could say His *Consummatum est*. Yes, all was consummated for Thee on the Cross, Oh Jesus! Thy work, sealed by Thy Blood, was accomplished; the Kingdom of God would extend itself even unto the end of time.

Oh my Christ Whom I adore! Thy Cross is the source of my Carmelite vocation; it is by the Cross and by Thy infinite merits which flow therefrom, that it derives its efficacious power in the world of souls.

'For what is a Carmelite if not a vibrant soul—one who has looked upon the Crucified God, and reflecting upon this great manifestation of the charity of Christ has understood Love's ransom and has willed to give herself to Him: a soul determined to share effectively in the Passion of its Master; having been redeemed itself, it longs, in its turn, to redeem others; thus it will sing 'God forbid that I should glory save in the Cross of Jesus Christ'. 'With Christ I am nailed to the Cross'. 'I fill up in my body those things that are wanting to the Passion of Christ, for His Body which is the Church'. (St Paul. Col. 1, 24)[51]

[51]Souvenirs.

'And to arrive at this transformation, to fulfill this mission, she must immolate herself. But she loves sacrifice, because she loves the Crucified Saviour'.[52]

My Christ, I love Thee; 'Lord, Thou knowest that I love Thee'.[53]

'Thy love has gone before me even from my childhood; it has grown with my growth, and now it is an abyss whose depths I cannot fathom'.[54]

Oh my Christ Whom I adore, Whom I love! Thou art my all, and I find all in Thee.

Thy soul is the divine book which teaches me everything....

Oh my adored Christ—crucified by love. To gaze on Thee is to learn how to suffer, to desire to be immolated with Thee!

To contemplate Thee is to understand the vanity of all that does not dwell beneath the shadow of Thy Presence. It is to adhere to Thy loving Will, to accept trials as a portion of Thy cross. To contemplate Thee is to purify my gaze so that it may become supernaturalised, seeing things in Thy light. May it view all the events of life from above, from the luminous summit of Calvary. To contemplate Thee, is to be enkindled with the fire of Thy love, to receive a drop of the Precious Blood, and with it the gifts of fortitude and of very pure love.

Factus est in corde meo quasi ignis exaestuans.[55] Oh my adored Christ!.... Crucified by love; we Carmelites have offered ourselves to be 'other Christs', crucified by love, with Thee, souls immolated to Thy Glory!

Our vows, doubtless attach us to the cross, but could one say these un-bloody nails are so very painful for the soul that loves Thee.

Are they not rather a means of liberation, love, joy, peace, ineffable happiness?

Oh my Christ, crucified by love, the consecrated soul, the Carmelite, will see beyond every trial Thy divine countenance

52*Ibid.*
53St John XXI, 15.
54St Thérèse: *Autobiography.*
55'And there came in my heart as a burning fire'. (Jer. XX, 9).

wherein she understands that suffering is a privileged sharing in Thy Cross.

'Knowing that suffering is a string which produces still more exquisite tones, the soul rejoices at having it on its instrument, that it may thus more sweetly move the heart of its God'.[56] These strains will draw from Him graces of mysterious efficacy for so many other souls.

What happiness, oh my Christ, to suffer with Thee and for Thee! Crucify me then, oh Jesus, in whatever way shall please Thee; Thou knowest what is most necessary and most sanctifying for me. Thou knowest that I offer myself as a holocaust to Thy Divine Will, and I embrace in advance, on Thy sacred cross, all that this Divine Will demands of me.

Oh my Christ, Whom I adore, crucified by love! be Thou the guide of my life, be Thou my All, my strength, my support, my light, my rest. *Suscipe me Domine secundum eloquium tuum et vivam, et non confundas me ab expectatione mea.*[57] On the blessed day of my religious profession, Thou didst deign to be placed 'as a seal upon my heart'.[58] May I ever repose, through all suffering and trial, on Thy sacred cross. Thus will this sign of union become a living reality. Take complete possession of my spirit and my soul! May everything therein be wholly Thine for ever!

[56]*Heaven on Earth* 13th Day.
[57]Ps CXVIII, 116.
[58]*Canticle of Canticles.*

FAIN WOULD I BE THE BRIDE OF THY HEART

Vulnerasti cor meum, soror mea sponsa, vulnerasti cor meum.
(Cant. IV, 9)

OH my Christ! this is the great dream, the ideal, the goal of my religious life.

To be a bride who rejoices Thy Heart.... what a plenitude of perfect giving, what a divine vocation, what a depth of union! To be a bride consoling the Heart of a God!—have we understood whither this reality is leading us, have we foreseen the summit to which we are called?

Have we fathomed, first of all, the depths of the abyss into which our nothingness must sink, so as to be carried thence on the wings of love, towards the radiant heaven of full union?

St Thérèse of the Child Jesus has expressed this truth exactly in the passage where she calls herself the prey of the Divine Eagle, and entreats Him to choose for Himself a legion of *little* victims worthy of His love.[59]

A bride of Thy Heart is then a humble soul, one who knows her weakness, and her powerlessness without the help of grace; a soul thus prepared to receive, through grace, the divine impress, and to be moulded according to the will and desires of its Heavenly Father.

The Blessed Virgin, our Mother and our model, fully expressed this double current of humility and confidence which animated her bridal soul, in her *Ecce ancilla Domini*—'Magnificat'! Magnificat! a bride after Thine own Heart, oh Jesus, will be

---

[59]St Thérèse insists repeatedly on this condition, which is indispenable to the union of love: 'littleness', which is nothing else than humility of heart. 'Yes, I am happy to feel myself *little and weak* in Thy presence, and my heart remains at peace.... I am too *little* to do great things, and it is my "foolishness" to hope that Thy love will accept me as its Victim'. (*Autobiography* Ch. XI.) Sister Elizabeth of the Trinity writes in the same strain: 'May He accomplish everything for us, for by ourselves we are too *little*, and it is so good to be the *little child* of The Good God'. Souvenirs).

then a soul of praise and thanksgiving, which glorifies God in everything.

It will be a soul of silence, contemplating with Mary the wonders of divine love, in the intimacy of the alone with the Alone.

But for a Carmelite—to be a bride of Thy Heart, oh Jesus, is it not even more than this?

Is it not to unite her will with Thine by love—so irrevocably that her 'inclinations and faculties may be moved in and by this love alone—Then the soul is so filled, absorbed, and protected by love, that it finds the secret of growing in love wherever it may be'.[60]

It is to give herself up to this deep contemplation into which Thou dost lead her, uniting her to Thyself more and more, so that she may make Thee more known and loved, and share to a large extent in Thy divine life.

It is to allow herself to be penetrated by the infused gift of Thy transforming grace, which invites her to the plenitude of union through which alone the soul may become, on this earth, Thy veritable spouse.

But before arriving thus far, the betrothed soul must sound the depths of Thy agony, of Thy utter desolation on the cross, of Thy Passion of love, suffered for the redemption of the world.

She must reproduce Thy long years of silence—during which the great harvest was preparing—she must follow Thee in Thy public life, by contemplation—beholding Thee speaking, walking, fatigued, suffering—always giving more so as to suffer more—and that even unto death—the death of the cross. 'For true union does not consist in delights, but in detachment and suffering'.[61]

She should feel burning within her that devouring zeal of Thy apostolic Heart, which was consumed with the desire to bring light into every soul, to preach the truth, to convert, to baptise, to fill Heaven with elect souls.... to undergo contradictions and trials of every kind and to offer them as ransom.

[60]*Heaven on Earth* 7th Day.
[61]Souvenirs.

71

Thy Sacred Humanity is and will ever remain my model and my example, oh my Christ! And I must espouse mystically all Thy silences, derelictions, fatigues, sufferings and death.

I must in truth espouse all Thy sorrows and derelictions. The sword of sorrow pierced Thee, oh Jesus, even unto the division of body and spirit!

But Thou dost count on future Simons of Cyrene. May I be among their number.

Oh my Christ Whom I adore! a bride of Thy Heart should allow her heart to be pierced by the lance of Thy love, till it also gives forth blood and water.

Blood and water—in the thousand and one little sufferings with which the way of perfection is strewn, and which Thou Thyself hast placed there as so many purifying and strengthening remedies, to help the soul in its upward progress along the spiritual road.

Blood and water, this sorrow (so often renewed for the soul that loves) of seeing herself so cowardly, so often falling, so seldom rising, progressing so slowly, and remaining alas! so far below her aspirations and her ideal!

Blood and water. This thirst for souls, which can never be assuaged, for it is as insatiable as the needs of sinful humanity.

Blood and water—some day perhaps a great trial, destined by the divine goodness as the means of making the betrothed soul take the decisive step in the path of detachment and absolute giving—the step which love expects. A great trial or wound, by which God takes upon Himself the work of making her share more deeply in His Passion.

In this Passion of love, oh my Christ, it will ever be Thy sufferings and Thy sorrows which Thy Carmelite will espouse; for 'he that seeks not the Cross of Christ, seeks not the glory of Christ.'[62]

So that she may not remain shut up in herself—so as not to suffer in suffering, the gaze of the soul must be always fixed above the limited horizon of her personal interests, upon the immensity of Thy eternal designs: love submerges all suffering, leaving only

[62]St John of the Cross: *Points of Love*. No. 23.

a profound joy at being able to give Thee to souls through her willing and generous co-operation in Thy redemptive Passion, through this efficacious response to Thy cry of dereliction.

In order to be a bride who truly consoles Thy Heart, oh my Christ, it is then in joy, peace and thanksgiving that I must envisage and realise my mission;'rejoicing at having been known by the Father, because He crucifies me with His Son; going to meet every sacrifice, with my Master, in the fullness of joy'; *servite Domino in laetitia*.[63]

Many souls, no doubt, call themselves Thy spouses, Oh Jesus, but very few are truly so.

For they bear Thy cross as if it were a yoke, as if they had no love—without that 'love which makes light what is heavy, and sweet what is bitter, always joyous, because always at liberty'.[64]

Oh my Christ Whom I adore! I wish to be for Thee a bride of light and joy, a consoler, who will sing Thy crucified love, renewing each day the symbolic gesture of little Thérèse covering Thy cross with roses.

Are there then any longer real sufferings where all is ruled by love?

'For love changeth all bitterness into sweetness—it exciteth us to desire always what is most perfect. Love feeleth no burden, thinketh nothing of labours; when weary is not tired, when straitened is not constrained, but like a vivid flame and a burning torch it mounteth upwards and securely passeth through all'.[65]

When, then, I view everything beneath the light of the burning rays of Thy divine Heart, oh my Jesus, I shall see that here below my path is strewn with nothing but graces, leading me to union.

Therefore—thanksgiving and joy!

Joy of spirit and joy of soul—so deeply founded on the joy of Christ that it seems to participate already in the supereminent peace of the beatific vision.

[63]Souvenirs.
[64]*Imitation of Christ*. Bk. III Ch. 5.
[65]*Imitation of Christ*. Bk. III. Ch. 5.

Joy born of complete giving, of oblation without reserve, of sacrifice which does not count the cost, but accepts all with utter generosity, finding its delight therein.

FAIN WOULD I COVER THEE WITH GLORY

Dominus elegit te, ut sis ei; et faciat te in laudem et nomen et gloriam suam.

COVER my Christ with glory!

This ardent desire of every apostolic heart is in the very framework of our Carmelite vocation: *Zelo zelatus sum pro Domino Deo exercituum.*

The glory of the Eternal—this is the supreme end of our life of union, of the spiritual ascent of every contemplative soul.[66]

Now, since 'Christ is in God and Christ is God', the glory of the Eternal is also the glory of Christ, and the glory of Christ is the glory of the Eternal: 'Father, glorify Thy Son, that Thy Son may glorify Thee'. (St John XVII).

The Word is in God, and the Word is God; and we have seen His glory—the glory which belongs to the only begotten Son of the Father. (St John I).

This glory of Christ is infinite, intrinsic, essential, as is that of God. And we can add nothing to it.

But God also enjoys an extrinsic, accidental glory, which He derives from created beings, and which is comprised in an eminent and transcendent manner in the infinitude of His intrinsic glory.

It is of this extrinsic, accidental glory only that we can speak both from the point of view of God's glory in us, and of the glory we can give God.

The more perfectly we reflect the Trinity, by sharing in the divine life, the more we shall glorify God.

That which will constitute the glory of Christ in eternity is essentially that which glorifies Him on this earth: the same knowledge—though in Heaven by participation, here below veiled in the obscurity of faith.

The same praise, with the same difference.

In us then, God Himself is His own glory, in the measure by

[66]St John of the Cross shows in his sketch of the Mount of Perfection, the 'Glory of the Eternal' as the summit to be attained.

75

which He communicates Himself, and according as He Himself is ours, and we, through Him, are His.

Since God has created all things for His glory, everything should therefore tend to glorify Him. At each moment, God expects this glory from our actions, sufferings, prayers, derelictions, transformed into the supernatural order.

This means that we must live in the atmosphere of eternity: we must leave ourselves, our own interests and petty preoccupations.

Tibi soli Deo honor et gloria—through constantly adhering to the Divinity who dwells in it, the soul will arrive at making the glory of Christ its sole object.

The glory of Christ is expressed here below in every type of sanctity but especially in consecrated souls, for these are created for the purpose of offering to God a ceaseless sacrifice of thanksgiving, praise and love.

And among these, who more than Thy Carmelites should cover Thee with glory, oh my God?

Sister Elizabeth of the Trinity has practically assigned this rôle to the daughters of Carmel, by desiring to make of her life and soul a perpetual Praise of Glory of the Most Holy Trinity.

Since we are not called on to preach, teach, tend the sick, or to exercise any sort of external apostolate in order to labour for the divine glory, our mission must take the form of intensified work in the domain of the spirit, so as to extract from our lives the maximum which God expects from them. It is then only by penetrating the inner secrets of our Carmelite vocation, and by remaining faithful to it even to the least iota, that we shall cover Christ with glory, according to our own special attraction of grace.

Then only, our prayers, silence, solitude, work, office, our fasts and penances, carried out with great love, will be transformed by the infinite merits of Our Lord Jesus Christ, into countless graces for souls.

For then we shall be living in our little interior heaven, where God will secretly accomplish great things.

Our Lord demands of us this particular kind of glory resulting from a life of loving union, and unlimited progress in the spiritual life, to the heights of which our life of prayer is drawing us unceasingly.

Other religious orders have been instituted to glorify God by making Him known in the perfection of the liturgy, in the austerity of their penances, by the rigid observance of silence, preaching, teaching and study; but for Carmel, particularly, is reserved the better part, *optimam partem*, invisible to the eyes of men, and not understood because it is entirely mystical: we have to glorify God by actually uniting our soul with His Divinity, by contemplation and intense love.[67]

'I wish to be a saint in order to glorify my Divine Master', said Sister Elizabeth of the Trinity.... May I no longer live except by love—that is my vocation.... all day long let us surrender ourselves to love, by doing the will of God, in His sight, with Him, in Him, for Him alone: let us give ourselves unceasingly, and in whatever way He wishes.... Let us live constantly—through all circumstances—with Him Who dwells in us and Whose name is Love'.[68]

Oh my Christ Whom I love! this is what I must strive for, for in this way I shall cover Thee with glory perfectly. As long as I do not fix my dwelling irrevocably in Thee, I shall live as it were on the surface; I shall be like 'sounding brass or a tinkling

---

[67] St Thérèse of the Child Jesus was truly burning with this seraphic ardour of Carmel when she wrote in the excess of her joy: 'Oh Jesus! my vocation is love! Yes, I have found my place in the bosom of the Church, and this place, oh my God, Thou hast chosen for me Thyself. In the heart of the Church my mother, *I will be Love*! Brilliant deeds are not within my power; I cannot preach the Gospel, or shed my blood—what does it matter? My brothers work in my stead, and I, a little child stay close to the Throne, and I *love* for those who fight. But how give proof of my love? Ah well, the little child will scatter flowers.... it will sing the canticle of love'. (*Autobiography*). To scatter flowers.... this is *sacrifice*. To sing the canticle of love, this is *contemplation*.

Mortification and *contemplation*, are the pillars of Carmel, as we have seen above. St Thérèse truly understood and lived the spirit of her Order.

[68] Souvenirs.

cymbal'; I shall be without deep love—without effective and dilating love.

As long as my soul lives amidst exterior preoccupations with any sort of attachment to them, it will remain mediocre and will not be able to cover Thee with glory.

For 'a Praise of Glory is a soul that loves Thee with the pure, disinterested love which does not seek self in the sweetness of Thy love; a soul that loves Thee above all Thy gifts, and would have loved Thee just as much even had it received nothing from Thee',[69] desiring nothing but Thy good and Thy glory.

Oh my Christ, detach me, purify me, fill me with Thyself, make me live to the full a life of prayer and union, which will glorify Thee throughout eternity.

Grant, oh Eternal Father, that on the day of my entrance into Heaven I may be able to say those words of Thy Beloved Son: 'Father, I have glorified Thee on the earth—I have finished the work Thou gavest me to do'.[70]

[69]*Heaven on Earth* 13th Day.
[70]St John XVII, 4.

I WISH TO LOVE THEE, EVEN UNTO DEATH

Deus ignis consumens.... Fortis ut mors dilectio.

I wish to love Thee—until I die of very love! To love!.... To love even unto death!.... Is not this the need of all deep love?

Love.... our poor human life is in some measure all caught up in this word which echoes throughout all creation from the highest to the lowest, the generator of life, of goodness, devotedness, suffering and heroism; the motive-power of the greater number of human passions, a flaming centre, flooding the world with the rays of its light, or its destroying heat.

If love were to disappear from the earth, then it would truly be an arid and desolate waste, a valley of tears, an insupportable place of exile.

But among all these human hearts consumed by love, how many of them beat for Love itself, the sole true and primal love —principle and end of all—the love which is God?

Among souls specially dedicated to this elective love, how many respond to it in truth—how many can turn in sincerity of heart, as did the Seraph of Assissi, to their Christ and embrace Him in a complete *Deus meus et omnia?*—'My God and My All'? 'For the sake of Thy love, I have suffered the loss of all things', oh my God!—lost all and gained all! Lost all that held me captive here below, and kept me at a distance from Thee; gained all the ineffable delights that Thy divine Love reserves for the detached and generous soul which it deigns to make its dwelling.

Now this is the sublime mystery of reciprocal giving, the soul, wounded by love, annihilates itself and forgets itself utterly in order to think only of its Beloved Christ—of His interests and His glory.

The heart, on fire with love, dilates all its faculties to an unlimited degree, its passions are purified, ordered, and disposed for the service of Him Who possesses and rules them.

The spirit, enlightened by love, thinks only 'according to God', it discards its natural operations, empty science, intellectual pride, all human accomplishments which sound wretchedly hollow and incomplete.

Even the body follows this higher impulse, losing its sense of importance—suffering voluntarily its part—which is a large one —in the redemptive passion.

God—Who is Love in essence, responds magnificently to love's complete giving. He introduces His bride into peace and into light.

Into peace!—*et pax mea exsuperat omnem sensum*—It is the Kingdom of interior silence, of stability, serenity, strength, unity, plenitude.

Into light!—into God's light,[71] where there is no longer any need of faith in order to believe and adore, where all is radiant in the light of eternal day—illumined by the rays from the Divine Countenance.

It is the Kingdom of uncreated splendour, of warmth, of life, calm and overflowing, as is God Himself.

The soul which God has united to Himself by this love, shares in the divine operation in the degree willed by Him. The more it keeps itself 'silent and solitary in love', the more will God communicate to it His infinite perfections, and the more it will manifest Him—thus fulfilling His divine purpose.

For we have been created 'to know, love and serve God',[72] and predestined to be made conformable to the image of His Son.[73]

Like Him, therefore, with Him, and through Him, we will love *usque in finem*.... even unto death!....

This is the crowning-point of love, the ultimate goal to which this folly of love leads us; and for a heart vowed to perfection this is not an empty expression.

Since devotion to St Thérèse of the Child Jesus has spread so widely, many of her devotees—not understanding her, entertain the dream of dying of love—thinking naively that it is so simple and sweet.

At the final moment, perhaps.... But to arrive there, the soul must have previously surrendered itself utterly; its will

[71]Colossians I, 12.
[72]Catechism.
[73] Romans VIII, 29.

must be sweetly lost in the will of God, so that its inclinations and faculties no longer act except by love. 'I do all by love; I suffer all with love. Then the soul is so filled, absorbed and protected by this love, and it finds the secret of growing in love wherever it may be'.[74]

Then, under the light of love, these little daily deaths-to-self —often so keenly felt, will be embraced with joy, and regarded as means of liberation.

For what often costs most is not the actual giving up of one's life—which must sooner or later be the lot of everyone—but the slow and continuous action of grace, which must destroy and pursue every imperfection to its last stronghold.

In the heart, in the soul, in the body and in the spirit, we must be always dying of love—and that, even unto our last breath.

Undoubtedly, for a Carmelite, love always renders the task less burdensome, for love is superior to life and death; it surpasses them. It fills with peace the heaven of the soul, and this peace overflows in acts of thanksgiving and joy.

'What souls called to the active life give by means of the apostolate and good works, the Carmelite gives in love. Hers is a "given" life, given entirely, an altogether heavenly life. In coming to Carmel, we have wished to pour out our soul as a libation of love, to break our vase over His feet, as Magdalen did, for Him alone. This broken vase, this ointment which flows drop by drop over Our Lord's Feet, is the life of souls who live in sacrifice and love'.[75]

For such souls, death can be only the breaking of a web, the crumbling of a wall, faith giving place to eternal vision.

May it come quickly then, this death of love—long and patiently awaited. May it come to gather the fruit which has matured and ripened by the destruction of the flower, watered by rain, strengthened by wind and storm, mellowed too by the bright sunshine.

May it come soon!.... and it will be the entrance into life

---

[74]*Heaven on Earth* 7th Day.
[75]Mother Mary of Jesus: *Foundress of Paray*. (Eng. Translation p. 126).

and eternal blessedness. It will be the dawn. 'I am going to Light, to Love, to Life', sang Sister Elizabeth.

'*In domum Domini ibimus*' said Mary of the Trinity.[76] 'Oh my God, I love Thee'! sighed little Thérèse. These souls indeed loved even unto death.

Oh my Christ Whom I adore! I wish to love Thee as they did. Fascinate me, so that I cannot wander from Thy light.[77] Teach me the secrets of love—so that I may love Thee truly— even unto death.

[76]*Life of Marie Antoinette de Genser*. P. Plus, s.j.

[77]The point is to distinguish the essential part played by the action of God, from the time of the soul's entrance into the passive way. It is neither the soul nor any of its faculties that act of their own accord, but God within it by the very fact of the active presence of the Holy Spirit. The soul then sees, thinks, loves, acts etc. under the impulse of God according to His own manner of working.

YET I REALISE MY WEAKNESS

Without Me, you can do nothing

THE soul which is possessed by love is necessarily a humble soul. One cannot attain to God except by annihilating oneself and recognising one's own wretchedness and poverty—This is the natural sentiment of anyone who is confronted by the majesty of God.

Moses—covering his face on the mountain;—the Psalmist singing down the ages *quia peccator sum—ego sum vermis et non homo—miserere mei Deus secundum magnam misericordiam tuam.*

To call oneself a sinner is easy—to really believe it is less so. Nevertheless one would have to be a monument of pride not to feel and touch at each moment, so to speak, the extent of one's impotence.

Inexperienced and weak souls, however, rarely escape a sense of discouragement when they become aware of their utter powerlessness to act rightly without the assistance of grace— according to the experience of St Paul: 'The good which I will, I do not; but the evil which I will not, that I do'. (Romans VII, 19)

This weakness, which was felt even by the great St Paul, ought not to astonish us, but should serve to deepen our humility. Discouragement is the daughter of pride. A virile and 'given' soul is never discouraged.

On the contrary: *Cum infirmor, tunc potens sum.* 'When I am weak then I am strong'. Strong, because I have sounded the abyss of my wretchedness; strong, because I no longer lean on such a miserable support; strong in the unlimited power of grace, which will effect its marvels in all their fullness, in proportion to the purity of my faith, and the extent of my confidence.

The soul which has really experienced its weakness, is a privileged soul, for then it will no longer be able to attribute to itself whatever good there may be in it or effected by it; it no longer cares whether it is blamed or praised, for it knows by experience how helpless it is without grace accompanied by the power of the infused gifts.

The interior movement of such a soul is ceaseless adoration and thanksgiving—thanking God for all things living, penetrated by the conviction that 'to Him alone belong all honour and glory'.

To feel one's impotence, and correlatively, to feel—more than any other soul, utterly dependent on God—is not this a fundamental quality of holiness?

St Teresa said that on some days she could not even pick up a pin without the help of God. And like her, St Thérèse of the Child Jesus was favoured—even to the end of her life, with great lights on her innate weakness and human frailty.

Is not the whole doctrine of spiritual childhood based on this truth; the soul's knowledge of its own weakness without the help of grace; complete abandonment to the working of grace—confidence that grace will accomplish everything for it, beneath the rays of love.

Sister Elizabeth of the Trinity, applying constantly the same doctrine to the interior life, wrote later: 'Yes we are weak: I would even say we are nothing but misery; but He knows that well. He delights in forgiving and raising us up, *lifting us into Himself, into His Infinite sanctity. It is thus that He purifies us, by continual contact with Himself.* He wishes us to be so pure; and *He Himself will be our purity. We must allow ourselves to be transformed into His image*, quite simply, by loving Him unceasingly with such a love as causes unity between those who love'.[78]

If then I am conscious of my weakness, oh my God, I thank Thee for this precious grace. If I fall repeatedly, if I struggle and toil without any apparent results, if I see in myself nothing but infidelities and back-slidings, if I know not where I am in the way of prayer, if darkness surrounds me, if I falter in the night, if suffering—physical or moral—crushes me and reduces me to nothing, if Thy merciful hand seems to lie heavy on my soul, my spirit and my body, in order to crush me and to make me like a beast of burden in Thine eyes, thanks, oh my God—thanks always! Thou dost treat me as a child of light, *secundum multitudinem miserationum tuarum—et exultabit lingua mea justitiam*

[78]Souvenirs.

84

tuam. 'The more Thou dost establish me in the knowledge of my misery, the more I shall plunge into the depths of Thy omnipotence'. The more Thou dost try me, the more will my faith increase, because it will pass over all obstacles to repose in the bosom of infinite love.

I BESEECH THEE TO CLOTHE ME WITH THY SELF, TO IDENTIFY MY SOUL WITH ALL THE MOVEMENTS OF THINE OWN

Induimini Dominum Jesum Christum
(Rom. XIII, 14)

CONSCIOUS of its weakness and impotence, the soul naturally lifts its eyes towards Christ.

He it is Who has willed to take upon Himself all our infirmities—*ipse vere tulit languores nostros*—'truly He has borne our griefs' and by His infinite merits has transformed them into graces of fortitude and peace.

From the Cross springs without ceasing the river of living waters which lead to eternal life, and these waters are graces of every sort, supplying all we need during our earthly pil grimage.

And Christ, our Christ, centralises and distributes them, because all flow from Him.

When therefore He will have clothed me with Himself—it is with all His strength and all His virtues that I shall be clothed in Him.[79]

[79]The soul which follows this doctrine of identification with Christ 'does not pursue such or such a virtue of her own choice.... but over and above all, the virtue which includes all others—a loving docility to the Guest of her heart'. (*One with Jesus*, p. 51. Père de Jaegher). 'The soul that wishes to identify herself with Christ does not invite Jesus to come down to her level by adapting Himself to her views and aspirations; she does not ask Him to unite Himself to her and to act within her, only for the purpose of helping her to live her own life more purely and more holily; she does not content herself with praying, suffering and loving as she has hitherto done, though with more intensity and purity of intention. Such spirituality would appear already very beautiful, but it is not sufficient, and in the difference we are able to realise the wonderful transforming influence of the ideal which we wish to recommend. In this second method of union, the soul thinks differently, loves differently prays in a different manner. For what she asks of Christ is to live His own life in her, and for His sake, not for hers. She wants Jesus to continue His own life within her, not to begin in her a new life which, though holy perhaps, would be circumscribed by the narrow limits of a puny

This is the great and sublime mystery of our identification with Christ and our transformation by Him, and into Him: mystery of faith which makes us understand the words of the great Apostle: 'I live, now not I, but Jesus Christ Who liveth in me'. *Vivo jam non ego, vivit vero in me Christus.*

'*Et indumento justitiae circumdedit nos: et induit nos vestimento salutis*'—says the Psalmist.

This garment with which Christ clothes us, is the power of His grace, the virtue of His justice, the splendour of His glory. For in every just soul, the special presence of God, *author of grace, is at once real, objective, and effective.* It is the presence of an object of knowledge and love—not distant but really present in us, and known, as it were, experimentally; says St Thomas.[80]

And when sanctifying grace which is in us, will have definitely reached its full development and consummation and is no longer in danger of being lost, it will become glory, and the fundamental principle of the beatific vision.... Grace is the seed of glory— *semen gloriae.*

Sanctifying grace may be considered as the two-fold movement of God dwelling in the soul and clothing it with Himself, and the soul letting itself be transformed by God, by not putting obstacles in His way, or hindering the working of the Holy Spirit: but rather co-operating with Him by a constant fidelity and by striving to intensify this life of union, and to identify itself with all the movements of the soul of Christ.

Oh my Christ! Thou hast called us to Carmel, so that by our union with Thee, we may draw down Thy grace on those

creature. The soul now stripped of self, makes room for Christ. She will feel the Heart of Christ beat within her breast; Christ will henceforth live His own life in her. She has made her own all the interests, views, loves, and desires of Christ, interests, loves and desires as far-reaching as the universe, and perfectly free from all self-love. To sum up: the spirituality in question does not only help the soul to become better, to purify herself, to find herself; it helps her to forsake self once for all, and to renounce her own point of view for that of Jesus. She aims at substituting Jesus for self'. (*One with Jesus*, p. 19 P. de Jaegher).

[80] *Cf.* Dist. II q. 2 a 2 ad 3 um.

whom Thou hast chosen to reproduce and represent Thee on earth; that by our fervour and generosity, Thy priests may be intensely identified with Thee, clothed with Thee, penetrated by Thy holiness, so that *Thou* mayst shine forth in them, always.

Grant that they may realise their great mission—which St Bernard compares with that of the Trinity itself: 'Creator, like the Father, when he consecrates upon the altar of sacrifice the bread and wine for the Body and Blood of our Lord; Redeemer like the Son, still on the altar—and ever will be until the end of time, *given* for the salvation of souls; Sanctifier, like the Holy Spirit, through the grace of his Priesthood and his uniquely spiritual ministry'.

After Thy Priests, it is Thy consecrated ones, oh my Christ, Whom Thou wishest to clothe with Thyself.

We shall not respond to Thy invitation and desire except according to the degree in which we are detached, peaceful, and solitary. 'As long as we prefer to rely on ourselves, and our will entertains caprices foreign to divine union—likes and dislikes —we shall not grow into Christ. He will not be reflected in us. For the fire has not yet consumed all alloy, the gold is not yet refined, we are still self-seekers; God has not yet consumed all our resistance in Himself'.[81]

In order that my soul may be identified with all the movements of Thine own, oh my Christ, I must contemplate Thy soul long and lovingly; so that I may find therein the example of all my conduct.

I must study this divine model, so that 'I may be able to represent Him incessantly before the eyes of His Father'.[82] Therefore I must strive constantly to forget my own interests and whims, in order to make the vast interests of Christ my own'.[83]

In difficulties, trials, in the details of daily life, in the duties of my state, in all the contacts of community life, in prayer; above all, in the giving of self, I will try to act always through Thee,

[81]Ruysbroeck: *Morceaux choisis.*
[82]Last Retreat 14th Day.
[83]P. de Jaegher: *One with Jesus.*

oh Jesus, and to identify my soul with all the movements of Thine. Thus, 'I shall keep all my strength for Thee',[84] 'I shall make unity in my whole being by interior silence, I shall gather together all my powers in order that they may be employed solely in loving'.[85]

'The divine light will then have so penetrated me that it will have made me resemble its inestimable purity; it will have *identified me with itself*, and will be, as it were, the life and soul of my spirit; I shall act only in and through this light, interiorly and exteriorly, in such a way that, receiving nothing from creatures and having nothing to do with them, this same light will preserve me in that purity which it has imparted to me— so that nothing may sully me, or even consider me save in terms of this light'.[86]

So then, I may hope to resemble the Son—I shall become His spouse—my life will flow from His.

My prayer will thus be recollected, my union effective, my charity perfect—proceeding from the very source of love itself.

'Though I may continually fall, in trustful faith I will ask Him to raise me, knowing that He will forgive me, and with jealous care will cleanse me perfectly. More than that, He will strip me, will deliver me from my miseries, from all that offers an obstacle to the divine action within me. He will draw my powers to Him and make them captive, triumphing over them as they dwell in Him. Then I shall have passed completely into Him and I shall live utterly of His superabundant Life'.[87]

[84]Psalm LVIII, 10.

[85]Souvenirs.

[86]Adaptation au Dialogue III. *Entrée à la Divine Sapience*, by F. Maur, p. 121 of the opuscule of Fr Pascal of the Bl. Sacrament.

[87]Last Retreat 12th Day.

In *The Life of Marie-Antoinette de Genser*, by Père Plus, s.j. we find a very suggestive passage on this doctrine: 'How are we to realise this ardent longing to possess God more and more—to give Him daily greater glory? Oh it is very simple; by living this life "in Christ", to which the Father has called us by the sanctifying action of His Spirit. Christ is the

"Amen", that is to say, the great Praise, the great Adorer, the great Apostle. What must the soul do—tormented as it is with the desire to procure by and around itself, the greatest possible praise, adoration and love of God? Simply—but what vast meaning is implied—to be "Christ" as fully as possible. The more one acts only with Him, Who is the perfect Praise, the perfect Adoration, the more one will glorify the Heavenly Father—the adorable Trinity.

Humility then—humility in the deepest sense of the word, means the disappearance of all within us which is not Christ, death of the miserable human ego, perfect realisation of the *jam non ego* of St Paul'.

IMMERSE ME IN THYSELF, POSSESS ME WHOLLY, SUBSTITUTE THYSELF FOR ME, THAT MY LIFE MAY BE BUT A RADIANCE OF THINE OWN

Trahe me, post te.... in odorem unguentorum tuorum currimus

(Canticle of Canticles)

Sicut mare magnum.... if the iniquity of man has been compared to the deep sea, surely the love of God, in an even more striking way, may be thus compared: this 'too-great love' of God which floods and engulfs the soul at certain times like the impetuous waves of the sea.

But that this complete invasion of the soul by the supernatural may be possible, all that is human in it must be destroyed: *the soul must be void, stripped, solitary.*[88]

Then the flood-tide of love will be able to penetrate even into the marrows of its powers, to fill it to such a degree that all that is yet imperfect, commonplace, natural, will disappear—so that that which is mortal may be absorbed in life.

'Thus re-clothed with Jesus Christ, the soul no longer has anything to fear from external contacts or interior difficulties. These things, far from being obstacles to it, only serve to root it more deeply in the love of its Master. Through all, and in spite of all, she continues to adore Him, always for His own sake.... because the Lord has hidden her in the secret of His tabernacle—that is, in Himself'.[89]

*She possesses God, and He fills her with His overflowing plenitude —'she is a reflection of all that He is—*as it were an unfathomable abyss into which He can flow and expand. She also resembles a

[88]'When you shall have begun to free yourself from earthly things in order to taste and relish in all your powers the fountain of divine pleasure, and to fix your will in God with understanding—the Holy Spirit will be your teacher, and it will no longer be necessary for you to have recourse to the teachings of holy scripture in order to learn in them the love of God'. (St Albert the Great: *Union with God.*)

[89]Last Retreat 13th Day.

crystal through which He can shine and contemplate His perfections and His own splendour'.[90]

It is an unceasing communication of light, warmth and fate. For the soul remains passive under the divine action, which likes the place of the action of the soul itself.

The Holy Spirit breathes freely in her and fills her with His light: The Father treats her as His daughter, and fills her with His plenitude; the Son, with His infinite perfections, takes complete possession of her, and so absorbs her into Himself that she becomes but a radiance of Him.

Does not this triumph of transforming love realise fully the words of the Gospel; 'All that is mine is Thine—*Mea omnia tua sunt et tua mea sunt: et clarificatus sum in eis'.*[91]

Oh my beloved Saviour, Sun of justice, Splendour of the Father, Thou Who dost manifest Thy life to the world and hast deigned to accept the oblation of my poor life for the salvation of souls, penetrate me so that I may become a feeble radiance of Thy own life.

> Radiating goodness, tenderness, humility, charity—
> Radiating light, strength, justice, truth—
> Radiating peace, joy, trust, and love.

Oh my Saviour, to radiate Thee—this is indeed the aim of my life as a Carmelite! To radiate Thee, by means of the mysterious stream of grace which overflows from a life entirely consecrated to Thy love; by the generous gift of self, amidst darkness, silence, self-renunciation, penance. To radiate Thee even by means of my darkness, offered in faith, so that other souls may be enlightened: through all my weaknesses and failings, which offer a two-fold prey to the immensity of Thy preventing and conserving grace.

To radiate Thee by my feeble praise, by the adoration of my whole being, called even now to sing with the angelic choirs the eternal Sanctus.

To radiate Thee by joy of spirit, by the supernatural activity of a soul which is filled with Thee—a soul happy to belong

90Last Retreat 3rd Day.
91St John XVII, 10.

exclusively to Thee, and to give Thee all that Thy love demands
—to find Thee everywhere, to see in the least of Thy wishes the
sign of Thy divinity lighting up the way. To radiate Thee by
truth and simplicity—by a holy liberty which attests Thy
absolute sovereignty in every sphere.

Finally, to radiate Thee, oh my Saviour, in the little circle in
which I am called to live for love of Thee; upon those around
me, Whom Thou dost wish me to love more especially; to
radiate Thee close to them is, moreover, to give myself to them
whole-heartedly, with kindness, goodness, serenity.[92] To radiate
Thee always in the degree and manner determined by my special
attraction of grace—by my supernatural vocation to glorify in
an especial manner one or other of Thy divine perfections.

To radiate Thee—even unto the hour of the great *Veni*, in
suffering and in love, in silence and in complete conformity of
my will with Thine—as a soul that is given, surrendered, no
longer belonging to herself—happy to immolate herself and to
'spend her substance—drop by drop—for Thy glory'.

[92]St Teresa puts at the end of the 7th Mansion of the *Castle*, this
advice to her daughters—so important did she consider it to be to avoid
those mystical illusions founded on a so-called spiritual elevation, without
the practice of fraternal charity: 'Be satisfied to help your companions;
this work will be all the more pleasing to God because you are the more
bound to it. Do you think it is a trifling matter that your humility and
mortification, your readiness to serve your sisters, your fervent charity
towards them, and your love of God, should be as a fire to enkindle their
zeal, and that you should incite them to imitate you in your constant
practice of the other virtues? This would be a great work, and one most
pleasing to Our Lord; by thus doing all that is in your power, you would
prove to His Majesty your willingness to do still more, and He would
reward you as if you had won Him many souls'. (*Interior Castle*, 7th
Mansion Ch. IV).

ENTER MY SOUL AS ADORER, REDEEMER, AND SAVIOUR

He dwells in me—His prayer is mine—
The prayer of Jesus, the Divine Adorer.
Mine is the twofold movement of his spirit,
Drawing me to the Father and to souls.

(Sister Elizabeth)

For I believe 'the love which God has for me'; I believe that the same love which drew Him down from heaven, drew Him into my soul, whither He calls me to dwell in Him, and He in me.... obeying this sweet commandment, I live in intimacy with God dwelling in me.

He lives in me. He is mine by sanctifying grace—this is the fundamental principle of my whole life of intense union.

'The truth is, God living in us.... Many baptized souls do not know of this interior mystery and remain unacquainted with it throughout their whole life. Deign to believe that the good God never leaves you as long as you do not oblige Him to depart from your soul by mortal sin. Make explicit, voluntary and frequent acts of faith in the real and constant presence of God within you. Do not search for God without, but within yourself, where He dwells for your sake, whither He calls you, where He awaits you—and suffers from your distractions and forgetfulness'.[93]

But in my Carmelite soul, Christ by His indwelling in me, must operate those things that pertain to the end of my vocation. In me, therefore, more than in other souls who are sanctified by His Presence, He will be Adorer, Redeemer and Saviour, so that through Him I too may be able to adore, redeem and save.

Since it is in the Holy Sacrifice of the Mass that Our Lord perpetuates His oblation in a bloodless manner, it is there that I

[93]Cardinal Mercier: *Retraite Pastorale*. Cardinal Mercier, when recommending his Priests to preach the fundamental dogma of the Divine Indwelling, named it 'the great Christian Mystery'. (*Vie Intérieure*).

shall unite myself to Him each morning, in silent adoration and atoning reparation so as to immolate myself mystically with Him in the Eucharist Communion. With the choirs of Angels and the vast assembly of the Elect, who have passed into Christ, I shall render homage to the thrice-holy God in Him and by Him; and by a deep interior perception I shall behold them 'prostrating, adoring and casting their crowns before Him'.

'First of all the soul should "fall down", should plunge into the abyss of its nothingness, so sinking into it that, according to the beautiful expression of a mystic, it finds the true, invincible and perfect peace that naught can trouble, for it has cast itself so low that none will descend to follow it. Then it can adore. Adoration! Ah that word comes from heaven! It seems to me that it can be defined as the ecstasy of love; love crushed by the beauty, the strength, the vast grandeur of Him it loves. It falls into a kind of swoon, into a profound and deep silence—silence such as David spoke of when he cried: "Silence is Thy praise". Yes! that is the most perfect praise, for it is sung eternally in the bosom of the tranquil Trinity. It is also "the final effort of the soul that overflows and can speak no more". (Lacordaire)....
The soul which meditates upon these thoughts, which understands their meaning with the "mind of the Lord", knows that He Whom it adores possesses in Himself all honour and glory; and casting its crown before Him, as do the Blessed, it despises self, loses sight of self, *and finds its beatitude in Him Whom it adores* —*whatever its sufferings or grief*—*for it has gone out from self and passed into Another*. The soul, in this attitude of adoration, resembles the wells spoken of by St John of the Cross, which receive the waters flowing through Lebanon. And those who look on this soul may exclaim: 'The stream of the river maketh the city of God joyful'.[94]

Enter me, oh Jesus, like this impetuous stream—this river of living water! Enter me as Adorer, Redeemer, and Saviour. Come! and help me to fulfill this great longing 'to offer unceasingly to God a sacrifice of praise—that is to say the fruit of

[94]Last Retreat 8th Day.

lips giving glory to His name'.[95] Make me understand that 'adoration in spirit and in truth', which my heart so often forgets. Make me recollected; penetrate me with Thy greatness during those hours of prayer when I am lazy, distracted, tepid, lifeless. Come, and teach me how a true Carmelite should adore during those blessed hours when Thou art exposed above the Tabernacle to receive the homage of our love. During these hours especially which so many fervent souls would envy us, help me to be completely 'about my Father's business', and not wander from Thy divine radiance. Help me to give Thee love for love, to become a burning torch, a 'lamp of fire' which shines mystically in the Church of God. Help me to adore 'in spirit', that is to say, with my heart and thoughts fixed on Thee, and my spirit filled with knowledge of Thee through the light of faith; to adore 'in truth', by my works, for it is by our actions that we are true; to adore in spirit and in truth by and with Jesus Christ.[96] For He is the true Adorer of the Father.

Adoration, reparation—prayer and penance—This is what Thy Heart asks of Thy friends and Thy chosen ones. This is what I am asked to give, in Carmel, the whole day long.

Our holy Mother St Teresa saw souls falling into hell like flakes of snow—and this frightful scene continues, is even increased by the wave of immorality, luxury and pleasure which is sweeping over the world. Are we convinced of this? Do we in our prayers, avert to the fact that innumerable souls are depending on our fidelity, our fervour, our generous payment of the ransom for their sinful lives? Are we concerned about all the souls in their agony, struggling and sighing after the final grace, which can be obtained only at the price of our sacrifices and sufferings?

Let us represent to ourselves this entreating army of souls in purgatory—begging us not to forget them so soon, but to alleviate their sufferings and shorten their exile by every means at our disposal—such simple means—and not much of a burden on our spiritual laziness. The treasury of indulgences is wide

[95]Hebrews XIII, 15.

[96]Souvenirs.

open to the children of Carmel—is it not? Shall we remain insensible to the cry of these souls who are expecting their final deliverance?

St Thérèse of the Child Jesus, in her picturesque style has described so well our vocation of love, reparation and redemption, in that profound passage where, addressing herself to Jesus, she asks Him of what use are her flowers and songs. 'Ah, I know very well', she says, 'that these frail petals of little value, these songs of love from the heart of one so little as I am, will please Thee nevertheless. The Church triumphant will smile on them, and stooping towards her child, will gather up these scattered rose petals, and passing them through Thy divine hands in order that they may acquire an infinite value will shower them on the Church suffering to quench its fires, and over the Church militant, that it may be victorious'.[97]

Like her, we can and must cast the flowers of sacrifice, adoration and reparation at the feet of Jesus. These fragrant petals will obtain life for countless souls. Like her, together with Christ dwelling in us, each of us must be a co-redemptrice, a host, a victim—a victim of the great unknown love—of merciful love, which will consume us without ceasing, 'letting the floods of infinite tenderness, which are centred in Him, overflow into our souls', so that we can pour them out over the world.

It is there, within us, in this temple where God dwells through sanctifying grace, that He wishes us to prepare the altar of sacrifice whereupon the divine substitution will take place. We shall furnish the matter for the sacrifice; He will transform it, and divinise it by His presence and His action. He Himself in us, will offer this sacrifice to the Father—paying no attention to our opposition and repugnances, suppressing firmly all that would be an obstacle to His designs. Should we not be 'consummated in unity', so as to work efficaciously for the unity of all— *ut unum sint*?

If He is not 'all' in us, how can we help to bring about that He will be 'all' in all?

[97] St Thérèse: *Autobiography*.

OH ETERNAL WORD, UTTERANCE OF MY GOD! I LONG TO PASS MY LIFE IN LISTENING TO THEE

Audi filia et vide, et inclina aurem tuam. 'One word spake the
Father, which word was His Son, and this Word He speaks
ever in eternal silence, and in silence must it be heard by thy
soul'.

(St John of the Cross—Points of Love, 21)

'In the beginning was the Word, and the Word was with God,
and the Word was God. All things were made by Him, and
without Him was made nothing that was made. In Him was
life, and the life was the light of men, and the light shone in the
darkness and the darkness comprehended it not. He was the true
light, which enlighteneth every man coming into this world....
And the Word was made Flesh and dwelt amongst us; and we
beheld His glory—the glory as of the only-begotten Son of the
Father, full of grace and truth'.[98]

Let us, for a moment, adore in silence the divine generation,
the essence of the Eternal Word whose ineffable mystery is
revealed to us by the Beloved Disciple. The Word is in God,
and the Word is God, and the glory of the Word is the glory of
the only-begotten Son of the Father. We cannot penetrate this
unfathomable abyss of the Blessed Trinity, but can only point
out some faint reflections of it. In the soul wherein the Trinity
dwells, certain of the actions and operations of the Three Divine
Persons reveal themselves—either one at a time, or simult-
aneously. God the Father infuses His power, His creative and
ruling action; God the Son His Wisdom, His regenerating Word;
God the Holy Spirit infuses His love, light, and all His gifts of
grace.

'It must not be held incredible that in a faithful soul which has
already been tried and proved and purged in the fire of tribula-
tions and found faithful in love, there should be fulfilled that
which was promised by the Son of God; "If anyone love Me....
we will come to Him and make our abode with Him". And

[98] St John I.

this comes to pass when the understanding is divinely illumined in the wisdom of the Son, and the will is made glad in the Holy Spirit, and the Father with His power and strength absorbs the soul in the embrace and abyss of His sweetness'.[99]

Thus, the soul in which the Blessed Trinity dwells, has as it were, an intuition of that vast immensity wherein it finds God, and whither He carries it—sometimes in an ineffable manner. All comparisons by means of which the saints have tried to explain this mystery remain obscure and inadequate.[100] The Word alone, Utterance of the Father, can translate for us this inexpressible reality, and make accessible to us, according to the degree to which we are called, those almost unexplored heights.

Audi filia et vide.... Hearken oh daughter and incline thine ear, forget thy people and thy father's house, and the King shall greatly desire thy beauty.... This command is an invitation to keep silence. Hearken, incline thine ear, in order to listen to the Word of God. He will not reveal Himself except to the soul

[99]St John of the Cross: *Living Flame* St. I, 15.

[100]It is noteworthy that mystical writers tell us nothing of that sanctuary wherein the Blessed Trinity is revealed to them. Human language cannot describe these sublime foretastes of the beatific vision. St Paul would not attempt to express or make known the *Arcana Verba*—St John of the Cross, in the midst of the fourth stanza breaks off the commentary on his Canticle, by giving his reason as follows: 'I would not speak of this breathing of God, neither do I wish to do so, because I am certain that I cannot. And indeed, were I to speak of it, it would seem then to be something less than what it is in reality. (*Living Flame* St. IV.)

The blind seer of the Order of Carmel, Venerable Brother John of St Samson is one of the few writers who have attempted to express this inexpressible reality: 'It is the fruitive unity of God which ravishes souls, in its superessential plenitude, wherein as we have said, the distinction of Persons is no longer perceived, but only the simple Essence, infinitely withdrawn from all that is, from all that is not, and from all that may be. In this state the soul seems to be quite rapt out of itself, entirely and utterly taken hold of by each of the distinct Persons, Who seem to leave their distinct operations without leaving their mutual repose and beatitude, which is their and our common superessential unity'.

that is detached and self-regardless.... Our 'father's house' is all that pertains to the natural life, of which St Paul says 'If you live according to the flesh you shall die'.[101] Oh Eternal Word, Utterance of my God, I wish then to spend my life in listening amidst Thy creative silence, to Thy colloquies with the Father. I wish that my 'conversation may always be in heaven', in the heaven of Thy glory, in the heaven of my soul, in the heaven of my heart. In this interior heaven, above all that passes, beyond this world and all its pettiness, cares and passing trivialities; with my soul firmly established in light and serene peace, from which view-point it examines and judges all unimportant details. In this sweet intimate heaven—leading to eternity! Soaring thither by a ceaseless effort of will. Compelling myself to bring thither all those other souls who are held back by a mere nothing. In this utterly interior heaven, with the 'Three', recollected within myself, having only to close my eyes for a moment in order to renew my consciousness of Their presence, and to be filled with strength and peace.

There was a soul who listened always with most faithful attentiveness and intense recollection to the utterance of the Eternal Word; a soul perfectly recollected interiorly, keeping all things in her heart. Silent listener of the utterance of the Word, Mary, alone with her great secret, Mary at Nazareth, pondering in her heart these unspeakable mysteries; Mary, journeying through Judaea, following her Son in order to listen to Him still more; Mary, on Calvary, still listening to Him—listening even to His *consummatum est*!

Oh Mary my Mother, teach me to listen like you, silent and recollected to the words of the Eternal Word! Make silence in my spirit, heart and soul, so that they may receive with perfect docility, the words of your Divine Son—you, whose prayer was uninterrupted; be for me the Mediatrix of all Graces at the feet of your Jesus, night and day. Oh Mary, *Mater Amabilis*, teach me to meet all things with a smile; to reflect, however slightly the divine gentleness and amiability, so that souls may see how sweet a thing is the immolation of love. Oh Mary, cause of our

[101]Last Retreat 10th Day.

100

joy; help me to rejoice always in the utterances of the Word, to sing His glory, and the joy which in Carmel blossoms triumphantly on the thorny bush of renunciation and penance. Oh Mary, faithful Virgin, in those sorrowful hours when I am asked to follow you to Calvary, be always at my side—close to me— *stabat Mater dolorosa*—in order to help me to receive from the lips of the Word Himself, this lesson of eternal life. Oh Mary, Queen, Beauty of Carmel, *Decor Carmeli, Janua Caeli*, at the final hour be with me still, and make me hear the *Veni* of the Beloved. Beneath your virginal mantle, may I pass into the bosom of the Father, where I shall hear for all eternity the voice of the Beloved, the Eternal Word.

I WISH TO BECOME QUITE DOCILE, THAT I MAY LEARN ALL FROM THEE

IT is not sufficient merely to listen—even though this is no small achievement, especially where there is question of hearing the interior call to the life of union. One must also become 'teachable'. From the human standpoint, this implies listening without bias, without previously-conceived ideas, without one or other of these defects of the will and intellect which cloud the judgement and hinder learning.

In order to understand the divine word which the Word wishes us to hear in union, the soul must be disencumbered of all that is not God, and must become humbly attentive, docile and recollected, established in a sovereign peace and tranquillity. It must be receptive, tranquil, peaceful and serene after the manner of God.... 'For the spirit needs to be so free and so completely annihilated, that any kind of thought or meditation or pleasure to which the soul in this state may conceive an attachment, would impede and disturb it, and would introduce noise into that deep silence which it is meet that the soul should observe according both to sense and to spirit, so that it may hear the deep and delicate voice in which God speaks to the heart in this secret place'.[102]

'A Praise of Glory', writes Sister Elizabeth of the Trinity, 'is a soul of silence, a lyre beneath the mysterious touch of the Holy Ghost, from which He can draw divine harmonies'.[103] No words could better express this state of extreme delicacy, purity and fidelity, to which every Carmelite soul should tend. For it is by contemplatives especially that the Word wishes His words to be heard—it is such souls that He wishes to illumine and vivify eternally by His 'secret touches', His interior enlightenments.

Again, 'a soul which listens to self, which is pre-occupied with its sensibilities, which indulges in useless thoughts or desires, scatters its forces. It is not completely under God's sway, it is not entirely docile to the teaching of the Word; its lyre is not in

[102]St John of the Cross: *Living Flame* St. III, 34.
[103]*Heaven on Earth* 13th Day.

tune, so that when the divine Master touches it, He cannot draw forth divine harmonies, it is too human and discordant'.[104]

During the hours which we daily consecrate to mental prayer, Thou, oh Jesus, do keep me at Thy Feet like Magdalen, seeking only the one thing necessary, listening to Thee, contemplating Thee in the sweet repose of love which constitutes the 'better part'. Grant me then the precious grace of becoming completely docile so that I may learn all from Thee. Grant that I may leave, lose sight of and forget self; that I may leave, lose and forget all creatures, occupations, fancies, temptations, sufferings, even duties, so that I may concentrate entirely on Thee, with all the powers of my heart. For it is during these hours of prayer that the Divine Word will imprint Himself in my soul—teaching me mysteriously, in the silence of the alone with the Alone. During these hours, He enlightens, reproaches, communicates His ineffable secrets. By contemplative prayer, we learn to know God, to become impregnated with Him, to penetrate into Him. Grace then works more powerfully, for are we not then more particularly 'vessels' which it can fill, and which will in their turn pour forth grace on the world of souls.

Never let us forget, it is from Him alone, our Eternal Word, that we must learn everything. A Carmelite will never find elsewhere the science of the Saints. In vain will she seek to enrich her soul with much spiritual learning—she may desire to appropriate to herself the writings of saints and scholars, but if the Word of God does not enlighten her in secret, she will never arrive at loving contemplation.

Oh my Saviour, my Eternal Word, lead me to the source of life, which is Thyself. Fill me, during my hours of prayer with the science of Thy love.

Make me, above all, quite docile, so that I may learn all from Thee. There will be hours of weariness, when the devil will make terrible assaults to distract me from Thee. There will be hours of darkness, when the sun of faith will seem to be eclipsed —in order to hide Thee from me. Hours of aridity—when everything will seem gloomy, difficult, boring, tedious—to keep

[104]Last Retreat 2nd Day.

me at a distance from Thee. Hours of heaviness when fatigue, drowsiness, illness, will get possession of my poor harassed soul—in order to crush it, were it not for Thee. Hours of struggle, when nature will rebel and try to shake off the yoke—to draw me away from Thee. Finally there will be hours of agony, when heart and soul will be broken by the weight of suffering—to make me weep with Thee.

Oh my Saviour, Eternal Word, Utterance of my God, in all these circumstances through which Thy love wishes me to pass, in order to co-operate with Thee in the salvation of souls; in these hours of storm and darkness, of doubt and suffering, I know that Thou wilt be there, always, and that when Thy voice makes itself heard above the waves, there will come a great calm—and this will be peace.

Peace—luminous, majestic, becoming ever deeper—so that my soul will be able to continue her office of eternity. Peace—acquired by meritorious striving—the peace of the courageous—of those who have fought a good fight, of those to whom Thou wilt give the palm. Peace—expressing itself in profound joy—joy born of divine charity; *gaudium quod ex divina caritate procedit—quidam est caritatis actus seu effectus*—of which it is both the act and the effect.[105]

THROUGH ALL DARKNESS, ALL PRIVATIONS, ALL HELPLESSNESS

The most important thing in the spiritual life, is to empty the soul of all attachments to created things, so that it may remain interiorly united to God and conformed to Him.

(Albert the Great, Union with God)

How well we know the struggle of the soul which, though tending to divine union yet remains human, always beset by weaknesses, imperfections, and the miseries of our poor fallen nature. In this interior strife, this tremendous conflict between nature and grace, one experiences the truth of those words of St Paul. 'For I do not that good which I will, but the evil which I hate, that I do'. (Rom. VII, 15). For the soul which has arrived at the threshold of union, the pacification is advanced, for here there will be no longer violent struggles and serious falls, but an infinitely more intense purification of the spirit. Sister Elizabeth of the Trinity has clearly indicated in her Prayer this progressive spiritual ascension. This phrase brings us to the Night of the Spirit, described by St John of the Cross: a night which differs from the first night, which is that of beginners. This is the Night of the Spirit, the painful darkness of the soul 'thirsting for the union of love', which experiences painfully the extent of its weakness: a night which can attain to such a degree of intensity as to be compared with purgatory itself. 'The more intimate and the more perfect the finished work is to be and to remain, the more intimate, perfect, and pure must be the labour; the firmer the edifice, the harder the labour'.[106] But in the case of Sister

---

[106] St John of the Cross: *Dark Night* Bk. II 9.

Inasmuch as God here purges the soul according to the substance of its sense and spirit, and according to the interior and exterior faculties, the soul must needs be in all respects reduced to a state of emptiness, poverty and abandonment, and must be left dry and empty and in darkness. For the sensual part is purified in aridity, the faculties are purified in the emptiness of their apprehensions, and the spirit is purified in thick darkness.... Here God greatly humbles the soul in order that

Elizabeth, this is where her strong faith, hope, charity and humility reveal themselves. 'Though I may fall continually, in trustful faith I will ask Him to raise me up, knowing that He will forgive me, and with jealous care will cleanse me perfectly. More than that, He will strip me, will deliver me from my miseries, and from all that offers an obstacle to the divine action upon me. *He will draw my powers to Him amd make them captive triumphing over them as they dwell in Him*'.[107].

This is the crucible in which souls are purified as gold is refined in the furnace. It is necessary that the soul should pass through this trial, in order that it may actually experience how deep is the abyss of its weakness—when unaided by grace—and how profound its misery. If it is the crucible of love, it is also that of humility. For the higher the degree of love to which the soul is called, the greater need there is that it should be thoroughly convinced of its nothingness, and this will only result from a realisation of its 'natural inaptitude for divine things'.[108]

The true lesson in humility—one never to be forgotten—comes from God. The higher He intends to raise the soul, the lower He abases it. Having first brought it low by exterior humiliations, He is pleased to take away from it, one by one, all the powers of the natural, intellectual, and even spiritual faculties. He thus leaves the spirit void, stripped, and brought to nothing, to struggle in the dark night, into which not even the faintest ray of light can filter. And, as St John of the Cross and all spiritual writers explain, the intensity of the night is proportioned to the strength of the soul, and the height to which God intends to raise it, and also to the degree of purification which the soul needs.

'When the just man dwells in the depths of his poverty, contemplating the nothingness and wretchedness that is in him,

He may afterwards greatly exalt it. . . . Of such are they that in truth go down alive into hell, for here on earth they are purged in the same manner as there, since this purgation is that which would have to be accomplished there'. (*Dark Night* Bk. II, 6).

[107]Last Retreat 12th Day.

[108]St John of the Cross: *Living Flame*.

when he feels himself incapable of progress or perseverance; when he beholds the multitude of his faults and negligence, he digs deep into the valley of humility. Falling beneath the weight of his misery, realising his distress, he exposes it before the mercy of the Saviour; he contemplates the grandeur of heaven and his own littleness. The valley deepens. And so Christ—the Divine Sun—darts forth a thousand rays and splendours from the height of His noon-day glory into the depths of this humble soul, so that it cannot help being touched. Not content with this, His liberality pours itself out, and overflows, for the soul now possesses the capacity to receive. That is why it is illumined by grace, embraced by love'.[109]

Then when the soul has suffered in this way, in patience and faith, it is confirmed in humility—as far as the perfection of a virtue is compatible with our fragile nature—and the Lord can put an end to the trial. It comes forth from this ordeal pacified, transformed, utterly dependent on grace with every fibre of its being. It sees things only from the supernatural angle; and in sincere and profound humility of heart, renders to God all honour and glory.

'What does it matter then, whether it feels or does not feel, whether it is in light or in darkness, enjoys or does not enjoy? It is struck by a kind of shame at making any distinction between such things, and despising itself utterly for such want of love, it turns at once to its Master for deliverance. It exalts Him upon the highest summit of the heart, that is to say, above the sweetness and consolations which flow from Him, *having resolved to pass by all else in order to be united with Him Whom it loves*'.[110]

People may judge the soul good or bad—it matters little. It may succeed according to human standards—such things have no hold upon it. It may be raised to extraordinary states of prayer. Instantly, and on every occasion, to God alone will it render thanks and praise.

St Thérèse of the Child Jesus has given us a magnificent

[109]Ruysbroeck.
[110]Last Retreat 4th Day.

example of this profound humility of heart, in the greater number of her last sayings. She does not confuse humility with a false sense of inferiority, but with her usual simplicity she declares that it is God Who has done everything in her—the weakest of all souls, and that in Heaven He will refuse her nothing because while on earth she was always faithful in love.

Nearer to our own times, and more renowned during his life, Cardinal Mercier, replying to certain people who wondered how his humility could survive the shower of praise, honour and glory of which he was the object during the years following the Great War, declared that he felt that all this was not addressed to him, but entirely to God alone—so great was his habitual conviction that to God alone belong all honour and glory—*Tibi soli, honor et gloria*. This indeed is the echo of a soul steeped in real humility, which Our Lord loves so much because it is nothing but the truth, as our holy Mother St Teresa says.

Oh Eternal Word, Utterance of my God, Thou wilt transform all my desolation, my darkness and my weakness into simple and true humility of heart—solid foundation of my soul's ascent to Thee.

I CRAVE TO KEEP THEE EVER WITH ME

Thine eyes imprinted upon me Thy grace.
(St John of the Cross. Sp. Cant.)

"THE soul which, by its far-seeing inner gaze contemplates God with a simplicity which separates it from all else, 'shines'; it is a 'day that uttereth speech' of His glory 'to-day'. (Ps. XVIII, 3). Night to night showeth knowledge. How consoling this is! My helplessness, my repugnances, my ignorance, my very faults themselves declare the glory of the Eternal!"[111]

And if 'I gaze upon God with that single eye which gives the soul a certain resemblance to the one simple Being, I can, through each one of my aspirations, movements, acts, however ordinary they may be, establish myself ever more deeply in Him Whom I love, and render homage to the Thrice-Holy God'.[112]

It is thus that I wish to attract Thee, oh my God, Eternal Word, to keep Thee ever with me by means of this inner gaze at once simple and profound, detached from self—so accustomed to live in Thy Presence that it is inseparable from Thee. To keep Thee at every moment of the day, by means of this ceaseless returning to the centre of my being where Thou dwellest. To keep Thee—by this self-less gaze which Thou dost expect from Thy consecrated souls—a gaze which becomes natural for one who loves. To keep Thee, in spite of my weaknesses—nay even because of them—for do they not give the soul that deep conviction of the little thing that it is and the little it can do, in comparision with all the graces which God showers upon it; do they not provoke a need of surrending itself ever more and more, and of rejoicing even in this frailty because by this means it can give glory to God?

And when my human eyes have the sweet privilege of gazing for a long time upon Thee in the Eucharist—by the vision of faith; grant that they may penetrate into the depths of the Light which shines forth from the Sacred Host. Light of purity, light of light, light of peace, light of love.

[111] Last Retreat 7th Day.
[112] Souvenirs.

It is by means of the Real Presence that every grace and perfect gift comes to me. The Real Presence, which we contemplate during hours of silent adoration.

Veiled Presence—while during our long hours in choir, the Tabernacle shelters Jesus the Host behind its luminous cross. Hidden Presence—only to be found by means of pure faith or acts of the will, in the sub-soil of the soul—without any sensible consolation—communicated nevertheless by the ardour of this same faith which transforms us into Jesus Christ, by keeping our inner gaze ever fixed on Him. The Real Presence, received, renewed each morning—bringing with It an increase of sanctifying grace, causing greater love and a greater aptitude for divine things—absorbing Presence which is relished experimentally in times of spiritual consolation.

Beneath the light which radiates from the Sacred Host I wish to live always—to live one with this light, in God—not in a transitory manner, terminated by the consummation of the Sacred Species, but in a permanent and vital union.

'Abide in Me', says the Word of God to us: 'Abide in Me, pray in Me, work in Me, act in Me. Abide in Me, whatever the person or action you are concerned with, penetrating ever deeper into this abode. This is the true wilderness into which God leads the soul that He may speak to it'.[113]

For if the soul dwells in Him, He will come to her and make His abode with her—the abode of the Father, Son and Holy Spirit. 'Henceforth the Divine Master has full liberty—liberty to infuse Himself into the soul, to give Himself "according to the measure of the giving of Christ" (Eph. IV, 7), and the soul thus simplified and unified becomes the throne of Him Who changes not, because unity is the throne of the Blessed Trinity'.[114]

This is that 'vast space', the 'nuptial-chamber', the dazzling light: O lux Beata Trinitas—Lumen de lumine—Lux vera—wherein I wish to dwell constantly.

If I strive to keep Thee ever with me, oh my Jesus, it is Thou

[113]Heaven on Earth 2nd Day.
[114]Last Retreat 2nd Day.

Who wilt fix Thy abode in me. Thy attributes and Thy infinite perfections will gradually impregnate my soul, imprinting themselves upon it so that it may resemble Thine. Then, the interior light will shine forth in virtues, gifts and graces. It will expand in strength, warmth and life. It will diffuse its radiance over souls, that all may be drawn to the Sun of Justice—'the true light which enlighteneth every man coming into this world'.

'A soul which thus permits the Divine Being to satisfy within it His craving to communicate all He is and has, is truly the 'Praise of Glory' of all His gifts'.[115]

115*Heaven on Earth* 13th Day.

AND TO DWELL BENEATH THY LUSTROUS BEAMS

Ad lucem quam inhabitas.
(from 'Sacris Solemniis'.)

'To contemplate the splendour of the Divine Being in His Own light, to penetrate all the depths of His mystery, to be one with Him Whom we love, to sing unceasingly of His glory and His love, to be like Him because we shall see Him as He is'[116]— this is the eternal happiness of the blessed. Can we not share in this happiness by faith, even while on earth, and begin, in the heaven of our soul, by contemplation, this unceasing praise for which God has created us? Surrendering ourselves, as did St Thérèse, to the 'Divine Eagle', we will let ourselves be borne away by Him towards the sun of love.... *ad lucem quam inhabitas.* There, we shall dwell beneath His great light—we shall be bathed in the splendour of His brightness, *we shall live in Him.*

Beneath Thy radiance, oh Jesus.... *ad lucem quam inhabitas....* what a sublime reality for the soul which seeks only the divine 'splendour of the Father's countenance'!

Ad lucem quam inhabitas! It is there I wish to live in spirit always, eyes closed, interiorly recollected, through all difficulties, trials and sufferings of earth—my heart in heaven—in the dazzling brightness of heaven's pure light. Filled with the fiery zeal which characterises the sons and daughters of the great Prophet —with heart beating only for the glory of God, and desiring with an intense desire to lead all the people of the globe to Him —longing to bring the light of truth to those that sit in darkness.

Ad lucem quam inhabitas.... ever penetrating further into the light, with the blessed spirits who shine in eternity: with all the beloved departed, re-united in heaven to the one great family which can never be dispersed by the separation of exile: with the angels, seraphim and cherubim. Our love, having become cherubic by means of the knowledge drawn from contemplation, and seraphic by means of the ardour of charity communicated

[116]Souvenirs.

by the Holy Spirit, we proceed indeed to the light of these blessed spirits who surround the throne of the Lamb.

Ad lucem quam inhabitas!.... with the Virgin Mother, Queen, Beauty of Carmel, who shelters us beneath her immaculate mantle, 'clothed with the sun—*amicta sole*'—beneath her crown of brilliant stars. In the apostolic Heart of Christ, furnace of divine love, shedding light on souls and drawing them to Himself unceasingly.

Ad lucem quam inhabitas.... according to our special predestination and grace—which love points out to us and asks of us particularly: hidden sacrifice, physical and moral suffering, self-oblation on the part of the soul, the spirit, the body and the heart; burning zeal, intense contemplation..... all these ways leading to the light, blazing trails which will be for many souls the way leading to the starry heaven, to the Divine Sun.

These ways leading to light, reaching out in all directions across the spiritual firmament—are they not, so many rays from the Heart of Christ, springing from Him, and returning to Him, in order to lead us, by Him, and with the Father and the Holy Spirit, to Life and to Love?

> *Duc nos quo tendimus—*
> *Ad lucem quam inhabitas.*[117]

---

[117] St Thomas Aquinas: *Hymn: Sacris Solemniis.*

OH MY BELOVED STAR! SO FASCINATE ME THAT I CANNOT WANDER FROM THY LIGHT

Sicut aquila expandit alas tuas, et assumpsit eam, atque portavit in humeris suis: '*Dominus solus dux ejus fuit*'.
(Deut: 32 10-12)

THIS prayer of Sister Elizabeth recalls the not less ardent cry of another Carmelite—St Thérèse of the Child Jesus. 'Oh my beloved Eagle', she exclaims, 'I wish to be fascinated by Thy divine gaze. I wish to be the prey of Thy love. I entreat Thee to let Thy divine eyes rest upon a vast number of little souls, and to choose a legion of little victims worthy of Thy love'.[118]

Thérèse of Lisieux has that devouring zeal for souls, as the keynote of her apostolate. In her thought and in her prayer, she never separates her vocation as such from the desires with which grace inspired her; and in this she is thoroughly Teresian.

Sister Elizabeth, faithful to her way, encloses her apostolate in the depths of union, which, by causing her to share in Christ's own life, makes her at the same time apostolic. She does not specify nor stop at particular details in the realm of the needs of Holy Church. She casts everything into the vast depths of the furnace of love. She implores the divine Eagle to fascinate her, so that she cannot wander from His light. For her that is everything: to dwell beneath God's radiance, motionless and peaceful, recollected, adoring, entirely surrendered—without seeking to know how or why—nothing except by love and in love.

A soul of one idea, her apostolate derives quite naturally from this state—and indeed more surely, for this dominating idea is the divine programme taught by Christ Himself, and commended by our holy Father St John of the Cross in his *Spiritual Canticle*; 'The soul which enjoys this solitary love may appear to be doing nothing', he says: 'but in reality, the smallest act of pure love is more precious in the sight of God and more profitable to the Church and to the soul itself than all good works put together. For this reason, Mary Magdalene, although she wrought great

[118]St Thérèse. *Autobiography*, Chap. XI.

114

good with her preaching, and would have continued to do so because of the great desire she had to please her Spouse and to profit the Church, hid herself in the desert for thirty years in order to surrender herself truly to this love, since it seemed to her that in every way she would gain much more by so doing, because of the great profit and importance that there is to the Church in a very little of this love.... After all, it was for the goal of this love that we were created'.[119]

'For me', declares Sister Elizabeth, all sanctity and apostolate is comprised in two words—Union, Love. Pray that I may live entirely beneath their sway, by abiding within the Blessed Trinity.... Since the Divine Master dwells in our souls, His prayer is ours, and I desire to partake of it unceasingly, remaining like a little pitcher beside the fountain, so that I may be able to give life to others by letting His inexhaustible streams of charity overflow on them.[120] 'For them do I sanctify Myself, that they also may be sanctified in the truth' (St John XVII, 19). Let us make these words of our adorable Master our own. Yes! let us sanctify ourselves for the souls of others, for as we are all members of the same body, we can cause the Divine Life to circulate throughout the great body of the Church, in proportion as we ourselves share in that Life'.[121]

Both Thérèse and Elizabeth have realised their ideal: to love God and save souls for Him. It is for us to follow the way which is most in accordance with our temperament and grace. For 'in My Father's house there are many mansions'. The way leading thither is but the form which is adopted by each individual soul, under the influence of the special grace of the Holy Spirit. St Thérèse is more of a realist, even in her vocation as contemplative.

[119] St John of the Cross: *Spiritual Canticle* St. XXVIII.
[120] Souvenirs.
[121] *Ibid.*

Does not this expression sum up Sister Elizabeth's life of grace from the apostolic view-point: to allow herself to be silently filled with love in order to pour it forth in an invisible manner over the world of souls: to remain like a little pitcher beside the fountain so that His life may flow into her, and she may pour it forth on souls.

Sister Elizabeth submerges all her apostolic ideal in the seeking of the one thing necessary—'a life hidden deeply in God'. And it is thus she surrenders herself: 'May I dwell, day and night, oh Eternal Word beneath Thy radiant beams—as the prey of Thy love'.

As the eagle mesmerises its prey, so Divine Love captivates the soul which desires to make a complete gift of itself to Christ, in order to be His instrument.

'Alas! without being aware of it, this soul will frequently fall back upon herself, and while believing that she allows Christ to expand His own life within her, she will in reality only be uniting herself to Christ to live her own life more holily. Instead of the great Heart of Jesus with its boundless desires, it will often be her own poor little heart which will animate her spiritual life. Unconsciously the soul will indeed often live not on the superior plane with Jesus, but on her own inferior plane. These two lives will cross each other, frequently intermingling but if the soul is faithful in rising again each time to the higher plane, if she does not cease to look up to her ideal, if she strives constantly to substitute Jesus for self she will some day attain the longed-for heights. It will require perhaps quite special graces, but one thing is certain—she will finally acquire that life more divine than human, the commencement of the heavenly life, the life of Christ within her'.[122]

Captivate me, then, oh Jesus my beloved Star! so that I may not wander from Thy light; thus I shall truly forget my own interests and be concerned only with Thine. Hold me captive from early morning, that I may remain buried in Thee in adoration, silence and recollection; at Holy Communion also, and at prayer, and I shall listen to Thy voice in the silence of a heart-to-heart intimacy. Hold me captive yet again during the Divine Office, that my soul may be united with Thine, attentive to the teaching of the Sacred Scriptures; give me to penetrate their inner meaning so that I shall not sing Thy praises with my lips only. *Da mihi intellectum ut discam mandata tua. . . . et scrutabor legem tuam et custodiam illam, in toto corde meo.*

[122]P. de Jaegher: *One with Jesus* p. 20.

Captivate me all day long, oh Jesus, and I shall remain in Thy presence, beneath Thy light, in the radiance which streams from Thy adorable Face, which will transform all that is not Thyself, and will lead me 'from light to light' to the Father's house.

Attract me, as Thou dost the angels and saints, and our little St Thérèse, oh Eternal Word, my Saviour! 'For Thou art the Divine Eagle Whom I love and Who allurest me. Thou Who, descending to this land of exile, didst will to suffer and to die, in order to bear away each single soul and plunge it into the very heart of the Blessed Trinity—Love's eternal home! Thou, Who, returning to Thy Father's realm of light, dost still remain hidden here in our vale of tears under the semblance of the white Host to nourish me with Thy own substance. Forgive me, oh Jesus, if I tell Thee that Thy Love reacheth even unto folly, and at the sight of such folly, what wilt Thou but that my own heart should leap up to Thee? How could my trust know any bounds?

I know well that for Thy sake the saints have made themselves foolish—being 'eagles', they have done great things. Too little for such mighty deeds, my folly lies in the hope that Thy love accepts me as a victim, and in my confidence that the angels and saints will help me to fly unto Thee with Thy own wings, oh my Divine Eagle! As long as Thou willest, I shall remain with my gaze fixed upon Thee, for I long to be *fascinated* by Thy Divine Eyes; I long to become Love's prey. I am filled with the hope that one day Thou wilt swoop down upon me, and bearing me away to the source of all love, wilt plunge me at last into its glowing Abyss, that I may become for ever its happy victim'.[123]

123 St Thérèse: *Autobiography*, Chap. XIII.

OH CONSUMING FIRE, SPIRIT OF LOVE.... [124]

Spiritus Paraclitus—Docebit vos omnem veritatem

Veni Sancte Spiritus.... Veni Creator Spiritus!.... how often we utter these invocations to the Holy Spirit, the Creator Spirit. Before any important undertaking, we instinctively seek light and guidance from the Spirit of God, from Whom 'cometh every perfect gift'. For without His grace we can do nothing—we can produce only works which are human and incomplete, if not useless and unfruitful. Above all, where our own sanctification is concerned, nothing will expand without a very special grace of the Holy Ghost. *Sine tuo numine, nihil est in homine, nihil est innoxium*—Without Thy divine gifts, there is nothing in man—nothing of any good.

With the Holy Ghost, on the contrary, everything becomes possible, everything is smoothed, corrected, unified: *rege quod est devium, lava quod est sordidum, sane quod est saucium, flecte quod est rigidum.* Guide the steps that go astray, cleanse what is soiled, heal what is wounded, bend what is stubborn.

Qui diceris Paraclitus, Altissimi donum Dei. Tu rite promissum Patris, Sermone ditans guttura. Thou art called the Comforter, Gift of the Most High God. Promised by Him Thou comest to bring us the power of speech.

Oh Consuming Fire: Spirit of Love! A Carmelite should have unlimited confidence in Thee, should have recourse to Thee at every instant of the day, for it is Thou Who formest her soul to the likeness of the Father, to the knowledge and imitation of the Son. *Gratia gratum faciens, disponit animam ad habendam divinam personam.* [125]

[124] Sequence for Pentecost.

[125] St Thomas Aquinas: I 45e ad.

'Moreover, the Holy Ghost is possessed by man and dwells within him, in the very gift itself of sanctifying grace. Hence the Holy Ghost Himself is given and sent.... Ia. q 43 a 3. *In ipso dono gratiae gratum facientis, Spiritus Sanctus habitat et inhabitat hominem. Unde ipse Spiritus Sanctus datur et mittitur*'.

Grace possesses the privilege of drawing God into our souls. The more therefore the soul comes under Thy action, the more grace will flood her with light and make her participate in Thy supernatural gifts.

Bonum gratiae unius majus est, quam bonum naturae, totius universi.[126] The treasures of grace are therefore superior to all those of the universe; for they place the soul under the divine influence, and make it docile to the Holy Spirit. They are the 'lamps of fire' of God Himself, 'giving to the Beloved the same light and warmth and love which they receive from Him'. (St John of the Cross—Living Flame, St. 111 77).

Lamps of fire!.... *Ignis ardens*!.... Truly Thou art consumed with burning desires for those privileged souls who yield themselves up to Thy action. Oh consuming Fire! I place myself beneath Thy divine rays, that they may penetrate me through and through, that they may destroy in me all that is yet natural and enkindle me with zeal and a very pure spirit of sacrifice. In the great work of growing in love, which is Thy work *par excellence*, I feel a continual need of Thy assistance—Thine aid, in order to know the way, and to follow it courageously: Thy light, to know myself, to see light in my poor darkened soul: Thy grace, above all, in order to see everything in the light of faith, in the light of eternity—always from the divine and supernatural angle. Again, I need Thy light, oh Spirit of Love, in the spiritual ascent of Mount Carmel, which is sometimes so arduous—especially when the soul reaches the threshold of the illuminative way, and still more in the unitive way, wherein Thy action plays the predominant part. For, *in order to arrive at the union of love, the spirit and the soul must be enlightened with Thy gifts of understanding and wisdom*, so that they may be made fit to understand, receive, and reflect God, by faithful co-operation with the grace of pure 'contemplation, which consists in receiving'.[127]

The action of the Holy Spirit is primordial in this state: He is the principal agent, Who guides and moves the soul, He will

[126] St Thomas 1a, II a q. 11 3a q ad 2, T.

[127] St John of the Cross: *Living Flame* St III 36.

watch over it continually and lead it by the hand upon the road which God has ordained for it in the perfection of the law of God and faith.... [128]

'Secretly and quietly God infuses into the Soul loving knowledge and wisdom'.[129]

'The soul now loves God, not through itself but through Himself.... since it loves through the Holy Spirit even as the Father and the Son love one another, as the Son Himself says in St John: May the love wherewith Thou hast loved Me be in them, and I in them'.[130]

Therefore I shall not cease to invoke Thee with love and confidence, oh Holy Spirit, the Comforter. Consuming Fire, Divine Paraclete!

Thy mission in the world of souls will be the continual fulfilment of Christ's own promise, and the need of our hearts: The Holy Ghost Whom the Father will send in My name, He will teach you all things and bring all things to your remembrance whatsoever I shall have told you.'[131]

'I will ask the Father and He shall give you another Paraclete, that He may abide with you for ever. The Spirit of Truth, Whom the world cannot receive because it seeth Him not, nor knoweth Him, but you shall know Him because He shall abide with you and shall be in you'.[132]

'He shall glorify Me, because He shall receive of mine and shall show it to you'.[133]

Do we Carmelites, souls of prayer, have sufficient recourse to the Holy Spirit, ever placing ourselves beneath His guidance, listening to His voice reminding us of the Eternal Word, thus becoming ourselves the means of transmitting this Word to all future generations? Oh Spirit of Love! with what ardour I should aspire to the plenitude of Thy gifts!

[128]*cf.* St John of the Cross: *Living Flame* St. III 29.
[129]St John of the Cross: *Living Flame* St. III 33.
[130]St John of the Cross: *Living Flame* St. III 82.
[131]St John XIV, 26.
[132]St John XIV, 16.
[133]St John XVI, 14.

The more I remain silent and peaceful in faith and love, the more Thou wilt fill me with these mysterious unctions, 'these delicate anointings which secretly fill the soul with spiritual riches and gifts and graces; since it is God Who does all this, He does it not otherwise than as God'.[134]

Thou wilt infuse into my soul the spirit of wisdom and understanding, that I may attain to the union of love; the spirit of fortitude and piety that I may persevere in prayer and overcome all obstacles that lie in the way; the spirit of counsel and knowledge, in order to see what God is asking of me, and to enable me to see things in His Light; the spirit of the fear of the Lord, that my soul may be steeped in humility, attributing all good to Thee, and realising that without Thee it is nothing.

Oh Consuming Fire! destroy and consume in me all that prevents Thy taking complete possession of my soul! Then, take up Thy abode there for ever; fill me with ardent zeal for the salvation of souls. May the fire of Thy love consume me, and shed its rays over a multitude of other chosen souls which it will offer as victims to Thy glory.

Thus shall I be a 'Praise of Glory, beginning already in the heaven of her soul, the task which will be hers for all eternity. Her chant is uninterrupted, for he is under the influence of the Holy Ghost Who effects all her actions, and although she may sometimes be unconscious of it (for human weakness prevents souls from keeping their attention fixed on God without distractions), she sings and adores perpetually, and has, so to speak, become absorbed in praise and love in her passion for the glory of her God'.[135]

[134]St John of the Cross: *Living Flame* St. III, 40.
[135]*Heaven on Earth* 13th Day.

DESCEND WITHIN ME, AND REPRODUCE IN ME,
AS IT WERE, AN INCARNATION OF THE WORD;
THAT I MAY BE TO HIM ANOTHER HUMANITY
WHEREIN HE RENEWS HIS MYSTERY!

Adimpleo quae desunt passionum Christi, in carne mea
(Coloss: I. 24)

In the solitude of the cell, or watching before the Tabernacle,
we aspire to the plenitude of the Holy Spirit's coming into our
souls with all His gifts. At the least interior prompting of grace
indicating to us the divine Will, we answer in all fidelity with
Our Lady of Nazareth: *Ecce ancilla Domini*. Thus will Sister
Elizabeth's prayer realise in us its mystical signification: 'Descend
within me, and reproduce in me, as it were, an Incarnation of the
Word.'

Some people may be astonished at this request, but the second
part of the prayer explains and completes it: '. . . . so that I may
be to Him another humanity wherein He renews His Mystery'.
In the secret designs of His love, God drew the soul of this little
Carmelite of Dijon towards the contemplation of the mystery
of redemption, viewed at the first moment of the Incarnation
of the Word, and granted her more than others a deep insight
into it. She tells us herself: 'I like the thought, the life of the
Priest and of the Carmelite is an Advent that prepares souls for
the Incarnation'. David says in one of the Psalms: 'A fire shall go
before Him' (Ps. XCVI, 3). Is not love that fire? And is it not
also our mission to prepare the way of the Saviour by our union
with Him Whom the Apostle calls a consuming fire? By contact
with Him, our soul will become a flame of love spreading
throughout all the members of the Body of Christ which is the
Church. Then we shall console our Master's Heart, and He will
be able to show us to His Father, saying: 'I am already glorified
in them'.[136]

The Reformed Carmel manifests indeed a marked tendency
to honour the mystery of the Incarnation—so little spoken of

[136]Souvenirs.

nowadays. Is it because the first Monastery wherein our holy Mother St Teresa lived, was that of the Incarnation at Avila? Or may it not be due to the fact that in the XVIth and XVIIth centuries, popular devotion centred round this hidden mystery? Or was the piety of our forefathers more theological than our own? Perhaps!.... Certain it is that few Christians nourish their faith by contemplating the Incarnation of Christ in the humble Virgin Mary.

Sister Elizabeth of the Trinity felt her soul drawn to this mystery by a special attraction of grace, since she delighted to contemplate that blessed moment when the Holy Spirit descended into Mary, and the power of the Most High overshadowed her, and the Word became incarnate within her. It was, moreover, beneath the supernatural impression produced in her by the contemplation of this scene, that she composed her marvellous prayer.[137] 'I need no effort', she declares, 'to enter into the Mystery of God dwelling within the Blessed Virgin; *it seems to resemble my habitual attitude of soul, and like her, I adore the hidden God within me.* When I read in the Gospel that Mary went in haste to the mountains of Judea on her charitable mission to her cousin Elizabeth, I can see her as she passes, calm, majestic, recollected, holding commune within herself with the Word of God. Her prayer was always the same as His: *Ecce*, here am I. Who? The handmaid of the Lord, she, His Mother, the lowliest of all His creatures'.[138]

We find the same idea expressed by Mother Mary of Jesus: 'Prayer during Advent', she writes, 'is to lean over the Child-Heart hidden in Mary, and there to find God's gift'. She was especially drawn to contemplate the first moment when the Humanity of the Word, coming into being, began to live united to the Divinity, and found itself face to face with God—in what humility, what adoration, and plenitude of oblation!

And in order to encourage souls to perpetuate the Incarnation of the Word, she said: 'A saint is a continuation of the Word, the completion of the Incarnation. The Incarnation is not yet

[137]Mother Mary of Jesus of Paray: *Life.*
[138]Souvenirs.

123

completely realised in all souls: it is not realised unless it is lived, unless we carry in our soul and in our body Jesus crucified. The mystical body of Christ will be completed only when the last of the elect has entered into heaven'.[139]

The mystery of the Incarnation, considered in this light, awakens the desire of immolation already expressed by the great St Paul when he cries: 'I fill up in my flesh those things that are wanting to the sufferings of Christ, for His body which is the Church'—*Adimpleo quae desunt passionum Christi, in carne mea*.[140] And this implies offering oneself, always and on all occasions, to suffer in union with Christ the Redeemer, so that His Passion may continue unceasingly in us, and this sorrowful mystery be renewed—this mystery which gives to the world eternal life. Unless the consecrated soul surrenders herself utterly, generously and blindly to the immolating action of God, according to His designs and for His glory, purely and without any personal consideration, it will not be void, and the Holy Spirit will not be able to descend into it in all His plenitude.

On the other hand, God hastens to enrich the soul which is stripped, and which has known how to break the thread which held it captive; it will then become 'a lamp enkindled in the splendours of the divine lamps, giving to the Beloved the same light and heat of love that it receives from Him.... even as glass, when the sun strikes it, sends out splendours likewise.... for although this is not so as perfectly as in the next life, the soul is, as we have said, as it were a shadow of God.... The will of these two is one, and thus the operation of God and that of the soul are one.'[141]

In this way the august mystery of our Redemption is renewed and perpetuated—the mystery of the hidden life, so appealing to our Carmelite souls: Bethlehem, Nazareth,—the thirty years of obscurity during which Jesus was preparing for His apostolate: silence, obedience, humble toil.

Mystery of the Forty Days in the desert: example of all

[139]Mother Mary of Jesus: *Conferences*.
[140]Colossians I, 24.
[141]St John of the Cross: *Living Flame* St. III, 77-78.

eremitical life—during which time God permitted His only Son to suffer temptation for our sakes.

Mystery of the Public Life—the labours of which we must endure mystically, in order to support by our prayers and penances those who work in the vineyard of the Lord.

Above all, the Mystery of the Passion, whence we derive, on the one hand, grace and strength, whilst on the other, we are specially called to suffer with Christ, 'as another humanity— putting our entire being at the disposal of Our Lord, that He may use it as He pleases—just as the Sacred Humanity was always at the disposal of the Word'. Finally the Mystery of the Resurrection which opened the way for Christ's coming into our souls. By our apostolic zeal, by constantly pursuing the end of our vocation, we must co-operate in this in large measure.

'What perfect manner of living is necessary in order to reproduce Jesus Christ and to act, like Him, only "in God"— that his works may be made manifest because they are done in God,[142] according to one of Our Lord's own expressions. It means we must set aside not only the influence of every irregular passion, but also all purely natural motives—in a word—to set aside the *human* and to subject it to the constant ruling of the *divine*'.[143]

'He gave me to understand', writes another Carmelite, 'that He wants me to be so completely transformed into Him, that the appearances only of my personality will remain, and may be to Him nothing more than what the accidents of bread and wine are to the Blessed Sacrament—that is, a simple veil, beneath which—even while remaining hidden—He reveals His Presence in a thousand ways'.[144]

It is thus that God will associate us with the divine Mystery of the Incarnation of the Word. Thus shall we be to Christ that 'other humanity in which He can still suffer for the glory of His Father, and succour His Church in her needs'[145] a humanity 'in

[142]St John III, 21.
[143]Père Plus, s.j.: *In Christ Jesus*.
[144]Mère Aimée de Jésus: *Of the Carmel of Avenue de Saxe*.
[145]Souvenirs.

which He can perpetuate His sacrifice of praise, and His life of reparation'.[146]

146*Ibid.*

AND THOU, OH FATHER, BEND DOWN TOWARDS THY POOR LITTLE CREATURE

Pater noster qui es in caelis

LET us recall to our minds the scene of the Last Supper. At the moment when He is about to consummate the work of our redemption, Jesus raises His eyes to His Father—'Our Father in Heaven', to Whom He taught us to pray—'Father, the hour is come: glorify Thy Son that Thy Son may glorify Thee.. that He may give eternal life to all Whom Thou hast given Him. Now this is eternal life: that they may know Thee, the one true God, and Jesus Christ Whom Thou hast sent'.[147]

Truth Himself tells us that eternal blessedness consists in knowing the Father, the Son and the Holy Spirit. 'Holy Father, keep them in Thy name Whom Thou hast given Me, that they may be one, as we also are.[148] Sanctify them in truth'.[149]

Now the expression of the Father is the Word, and 'to all those that receive Him, He gives power to be made the sons of God'.[150] 'Father, I will that where I am, they also whom Thou hast given Me may be with Me, that they may see My glory which Thou has given Me, because Thou has loved Me before the creation of the world. Just Father, the world hath not known Thee, but I have known Thee, and these have known that Thou hast sent Me. I have made known Thy name to them and will make it known; that the love wherewith Thou hast loved Me may be in them, and I in them'.[151]

This sublime prayer of Jesus to His Father is the expression of all that the soul which is called to the love of the Father and the Son should be unceasingly breathing forth. The glory of the Father's name, the coming of His Kingdom—these are the

[147] St John XVII, 1, 2, 3.
[148] St John XVII, 11.
[149] St John XVII, 17.
[150] St John I, 1.
[151] St John XVII, 24–26.

primary and essential petitions of the *Pater Noster*—and for a Carmelite the immediate objective of her life of sacrifice.

To know God, and to love Him—is not this the end of our prayer and life of union? To establish oneself ever more deeply in this union, *ut unum sint. . . . consummatum in unum. . . .* this is the ideal which we strive to attain and to make more perfect each day. To the Carmelite, as to Christ, is entrusted a multitude of souls, which He asks her to 'keep', save, and sanctify. Within our mystical enclosure, are our bishops, priests, missionaries, our families, friends, sinners known and unknown—whom the sovereign mercy of God has entrusted to our spiritual keeping.

'Holy Father, keep them in Thy name Whom Thou hast given Me'. May not one of them be lost through my negligence, tepidity, or lack of love.

'Just Father, sanctify them in truth'. Enlighten their souls with the Sun of Justice, that 'they may walk before Thee and be perfect'.

May I sanctify myself for them, unceasingly. Whenever I let myself become the slave of routine, when I follow Thee without generosity—not keeping before my eyes the souls Thou hast entrusted to my keeping—grace will be less abundant in them, and I shall be responsible for their faults and failings. If that intimate union to which Thou hast called me is not as intense as it ought to be—I shall be forsaking Thy dwelling, and the divine sap will no longer flow abundantly through the withered and stunted branch which my soul offers to the True Vine. The leaves and fruits which I should produce will wither and fall—and Thy paternal Heart will weep over Thy child.

Oh Father, bend down then to Thy poor little creature. . . . Forgetting those attributes expressing Thy grandeur, Thy immensity and Thy power, I wish, at the moment, to see in Thee only My Father, Father of all good, *bonus es tu*[152] Father of Christ Whose Heart is a burning furnace of love, Father of the Prodigal Son—opening wide Thy arms of mercy and pardon. . . . heaping Thy riches upon the erring child more than on him who

[152]Psalm 118.

128

had always been faithful to Thee.... All that is mine is thine....
Omnia mea tua sunt.[153]

Forgive me, oh Father, for having responded so poorly to Thy
loving designs on my soul—for having so many times resisted
Thy divine inspirations, and neglected Thy preventing graces.

Forgive me for not having understood the splendour of the
gift Thou hast revealed to me—for having strayed into the
domain of the mediocre, common place, and less perfect....
miserere mei secundum eloquium tuum.[154]

Forgive me for retaining even in the cloister a remnant of the
spirit of the world—the world which hates Thee, and has never
known Thee: for remaining attached to creatures and trifles when
Thou shouldst be my sole attraction: for having brought into
the religious life a multitude of imperfections, and not having
embraced once and for all the naked cross.

Forgive me for having lived without sufficient ardour, without
vast desires, without burning zeal: for not having understood
the value of humiliation, failure, suffering and dereliction—
Bonum mihi quia humiliasti me (Ps. 118, 71).

Forgive me for having left Thee solitary in my soul, and not
fixing my dwelling there *ab intus*, in Thy divine company with
the Son and Holy Spirit.... *Prope es tu, Domine.* (Ps. 118, 151).

Oh Father, it is there that Thou awaitest me, now and always;
there Thou deignest to descend and to bend over Thy poor little
creature, and to see in her only Thy Beloved Son in Whom
Thou art well-pleased.

I throw myself then into Thy arms—wide open to receive me
oh Father, and I will repose upon Thy divine bosom whence
issues all creation, all begetting, all souls. Thou hast ordained
that they should return to Thee for ever, *increatus Pater, increatus
Filius, increatus Spiritus Sanctus.*

I wish to dwell in Thy presence, beneath Thy gaze, which like
that of an eagle 'searches the mind and heart'.... And Thou wilt
fill me with Thy overflowing joy, and wilt come to me and take

[153]St John XVII, 10.
[154]Psalm 118.

129

up Thy abode in me.... and I shall repose beneath the shadow of Thy wings.

'My Beloved.... the silent music.

The sounding solitude.

The supper that recreates and enkindles love'.[155]

Circum duxit me et docuit; et custodivit quasi pupillam oculi sui.[156]

[155]St John of the Cross: *Spiritual Canticle* St. XIV and XV.
[156]Deuteronomy XXXII, 10.

BEHOLD IN HER NONE OTHER THAN THY BELOVED SON, IN WHOM THOU HAST SET ALL THY PLEASURE

Hic est Filius meus dilectus in quo mihi bene complacui.

OH Father, why this tenderness, this merciful forgiveness to each ungrateful soul? It is because Thou wishest to see in them none other than Jesus, Thy Beloved Son.

Thy indwelling by grace in every baptized soul is indeed the endless receiving of that mystic descent operated on the soul of Christ after His baptism and on Thabor. The Apostles could not bear the light of Thy splendour. If it were not to glorify Thyself, oh Father, in glorifying Thy Son, how couldst Thou abase Thyself, to Thy sinful creature?

When Peter, James and John heard the divinity of Christ proclaimed, and beheld in the cloud Moses and Elias bearing testimony to the prodigy, it was for them the unique vision, resplendent with the glory of their Master. This was 'Thabor'— perfect joy, ecstasy of love, heaven opened, displaying realities which no tongue could ever express. And the memory of this immortal hour, which revealed to them the divine filiation of Jesus, was to be shortly afterwards the support of their wavering faith in the Praetorium and on Calvary.

Thus it is with all efficacious grace. When we are flooded with light, this is in order that we may store up strength, faith and love against the day of trial and warfare, by means of which we shall give proof—either in actual reality, or mystically—of our unshaken trust in the eternal omnipotence of our Beloved. When God deigns to reveal Himself, in one way or another, it is to call us higher, closer to His Heart, closer to His Cross, and often *on* to His Cross. When He lifts a corner of the veil which hides Him from our darkened sight, it is to carry us into Himself, into the serene and intimate depths of love; but this will only be effected by means of detachment and suffering: our soul can only rise *per passionem ad gloriam.*

Therefore, oh Father, in the struggles and agonies of our frail human nature, as also in the serene triumphs of divine grace, deign to behold in our soul none other than Thy Beloved Son in Whom Thou art well pleased. And since, in spite of my frailty *Thou hast truly called me to reproduce Christ*, to be simply a living image of Thy only Son.... *I shall soon disappear, in Thy eyes, and He alone will remain*—He and the spirit of Love.

I shall then have passed completely into the soul of my Christ and He will clothe me with Himself. He will make me live like the Father in an eternal present, without past and without future, but wholly in the unity of my being, in this eternal 'now'. He will be my peace, He will give me access to the Father.—He will keep me changeless and peaceful in His presence, as though my soul were already in eternity. And I shall be pure and irreprehensible in the eyes of the Father, for my miseries will be covered with the mantle of His glory: and my countenance will shine with the hidden radiance of the face of Jesus. [157]

How ineffably, then, oh Father, wilt Thou bend over Thy poor little creature, Whom Thou lovest with an eternal love! Thou wilt come to take her and bear her away to Thy eternal mansions, where 'in Thy light she will see light'. [158]

Thou wilt create within her a new heart, a pure heart, a heart overflowing with holy joy, a heart that will sing unceasingly the eternal hymn of praise and thanksgiving: *Sanctus, Sanctus, Sanctus, Dominus Deus Sabaoth.*

[157] Souvenirs.
[158] Last Retreat 14th Day.

OH MY THREE, MY ALL, MY BEATITUDE, INFINITE SOLITUDE, IMMENSITY WHEREIN I LOSE MYSELF

In the heaven of our soul, let us be a Praise of Glory to the Blessed Trinity
(Sister Elizabeth of the Trinity)

THE soul arrived at the union of love is actually possessed by the Father, the Son, and the Holy Spirit. Behold the term of our spiritual ascent—oh my Three, my All, my Beatitude! This is the eternal hymn of praise and thanksgiving which the soul transformed into God intones on the threshold of eternity. Oh my Three! Father, Son and Holy Spirit! Thou livest in me, Thou enfoldest me in Thy invisible presence, Thou dost infuse into me abundantly Thy all-powerful grace—provided I am not like the inconsistent householder who abandons his own dwelling.

Oh my Three! my divine Counsellor, when I close my eyes to the vain disturbances of this world and creatures, I shall find Thee in the inmost centre of my being, in that interior heaven where Thou deignest to dwell, and then, with Sister Elizabeth I shall be able to say: 'I have found heaven already, for heaven is God, and God is in my soul'.

Oh my Three! Keep me well enclosed in this interior heaven; guard all approaches, for my recollection is still so unstable that a mere nothing often suffices to trouble and dissipate it. Keep my soul motionless and peaceful, as though it were already in eternity, so that it may adore Thee continually, oh my Three, and all its faculties may sing Thy glory in an uninterrupted canticle of praise.

Oh my All! How apt is this title by which I lovingly invoke Thee, for Thou hast entirely taken the place of self in me, and hast surpassed all the desires of this poor heart. In Carmel, where solitude and separation are so fundamental, it is good to feel this divine 'All' taking possession of me ever more and more, and gradually filling my whole being, and overflowing it.

From the human point of view, as the years pass, so do the

gulfs widen around us. The Carmelite plunges into a voluntary forgetfulness, where everything combines to bring about that people drift away from her, isolated as she is from the rest of mortals by time and distance, grilles and veils. After some time she becomes, as it were, dead while yet living, and the memories of the past becoming more and more hazy, will seldom recur to the mind, except in what concerns her nearest relatives. And this is as it should be. Thus has the Carmelite wished it, because God asked of her this total sacrifice, this absolute renunciation of the least attachment which kept her tied to the world— whether in spirit, heart or soul. 'For His sake, and in order that I may incessantly adore Him, I have isolated, separated, stripped myself of all things natural and supernatural'.[159]

In the monastery itself, the supports of our first days disappear one by one, or hide themselves; the affections become super-naturalized, and the more faithfully the soul responds to the divine action and its demands, the more it detaches itself from everything, to live alone with the Alone. 'This life of intimacy with God costs. Having paid the contribution of silence, one must pay that of absolute detachment'.[160]

Often, God permits the soul to find itself even without a spiritual guide, at the very moment when the solitude in and around it has become very intense. This perhaps is a supereminent grace, even though it is often a bitter suffering. The human heart is always seeking for a support, the human soul remains frail, and longs to unburden itself, to expand, to feel that it is understood, supported, enlightened, urged on—even approved of at times. And to find itself alone, or rather solitary on the spiritual ascent, in rugged paths, or perhaps on the heights, causes it an indefinable feeling of its nothingness and littleness. It is overpowered by the dizziness of the heights where naught exists save the Divine Immensity, in which all else is absorbed.

At this culminating point of its spiritual life, the soul realises the extent of the total giving of itself, the plenitude of renunciation, to which, step by step, God has led it. He alone remains to

159Last Retreat 10th Day.
160Père Plus, s.j.: *To Live with God.*

her and is her All. He, the infinitely tender Father, the Spouse of blood and of love, the Consoling Spirit, illuming with beatific light the noon-day and the evening of the unitive life.

While awaiting in peace and serenity the great *Veni*, the soul can sing in truth: *Tuus sum ego....* I am all Thine.... and Thou art all mine.... God having stripped, delivered and freed his creature, it is disposed to ascend by steps, to pass from this vale of tears to the place which is its end—that is from all that is less than God, that 'large place' which is the unfathomable Trinity: *immensus Pater, immensu: Filius, immensus Spiritus Sanctus.*[161]

'The Creator, seeing that silence reigns within His creature, who is deeply recollected in her interior solitude, greatly desires her beauty. He leads her into that immense and infinite solitude, into that "large place", of which the Psalmist sings, which is His very Self: "I will enter into the powers of the Lord" (Ps. LXX, 16) "I will lead her into solitude and there I will speak to her heart" (Osee II, 14). The soul has now entered that vast solitude where God will make His voice heard. "The Word of God is living and effectual, and more piercing than any two-edged sword, and reaching unto the division of the soul and the spirit, of the joints also and the marrow" (Heb. IV, 12). It is then, this Word itself which will finish the work of stripping the soul, its characteristic and peculiar property being to effect and create what it makes known, provided the soul yields its consent'.[162]

Then 'it rises, ascending above the senses, above nature, above itself. It passes beyond all joy, and all sorrow, passes through all things, never to rest until it has penetrated *within* Him Whom it loves, Who will give it the "repose of the Abyss".'[163]

Oh my Three, my All, my Beatitude, infinite solitude, Immensity wherein I lose myself.... this is indeed the song of this solitary and stripped soul, in its mysterious and divine ascent! For the solitude which is filled with God, is radiant with celestial joy—'it blossoms—it brings forth lilies'. What pure

[161] Last Retreat 16th Day.
[162] *Ibid.* 11th Day.
[163] *Ibid.* 16th Day.

joy inundates our cloisters! What inspired writer can ever tell of their quiet calm, their deep serenity!

To the eyes of the world, monasteries may appear as gloomy prisons, where boredom reigns supreme. But the world does not understand the peace of Christ, and the invariable happiness of those whose sole occupation is to love God.... *Deus qui laetificat juventutem meam.*

Here is already the hundred-fold promised on this earth: the bare cell seems more inviting than the most sumptuous apartment, for the soul who lives in it dwells amid the undreamt-of splendours of the other world. Its gaze is fixed on heaven, and its thoughts are above the mere circumstances with which it is surrounded. It understands the infinitude of the divine attributes, and realises their sanctifying effect. It no longer considers the details of its sacrifices, for its zeal espouses the interests of God in totality. Its love is the burning flame springing from Love itself, ever returning to its source in order to be nourished unceasingly there—mingling and losing itself in these sacred depths.

This is the plentitude of life in Unity: *it is loving fellowship with the 'Three'* and no one can rob the soul on these summits of its celestial joy: *Mons Carmeli, mons in quo beneplacitum est habitare in eo, cum Deo*; and in this infinite solitude where naught is heard but the echo of the Eternal Word, it embraces the All of God. On all sides, it is surrounded with immensity—unfathomable immensity—image of eternity.

Oh infinite solitude! Immensity of my God, wherein I lose myself like the most imperceptible drop of water, or bubble of air, may I plunge myself for ever into Thy depths like Sister Elizabeth and sing with her:

> 'I have found my centre in the divine abyss,
> My soul reposes in this Immensity,
> And dwells there with its God, as in eternity'.[164]

'It is there, sunk to its lowest depths, that the abyss of our nothingness will find itself face to face with the abyss of the mercy, with the immensity of the All of God. There shall we

[164]*Poems of Sr Elizabeth.*

find the strength to die to self, and losing all trace of self, we shall be transformed in love—Blessed are they who die in the Lord'.[165]

[165]*Heaven on Earth* 2nd Day.

I YIELD MYSELF TO THEE AS THY PREY

Dirupisti Domine, vincula mea. Tibi sacrificabo hostiam laudis

'I long to be *fascinated* by Thy divine eyes, oh my Divine Eagle, I long to become the prey of Thy Love. I am filled with the hope that one day Thou wilt swoop down upon me, and bearing me away to the source of all love wilt plunge me at last into its glowing abyss, that I may become for ever its happy victim'.166

Following the example of little St Thérèse, how many souls, oh Jesus, have made this sublime offering—but do they really understand what it implies? To be Thy prey—this is the consummation of the holocaust, the gift of martyrdom; it is to be the 'wheat of Christ' which St Ignatius of Antioch longed to become. It is blood, anguish, the heroic death of all the martyrs, of ancient and modern times. It is the daily, slow crucifixions of hidden martyrs of illness, devotion to duty, missionary work in lands of burning heat, swamp, and ice. It is the gift of self, of all apostolates spiritual and moral; zeal, preaching, charity under every form. It is the prolonged spending—more hidden and more unknown—of lives vowed to contemplation and penance— 'distilling all their substance, drop by drop' for the glory of God.

But, generally speaking, the prey is captured without delay, borne off, crushed, consumed. The soul which has arrived at the union of love, longs only for fusion, for the consummation of union in glory. This often gives rise to a desire for martyrdom's heroic offering—an attraction which the Holy Spirit infuses into the soul.

Let us listen to Théophane Vénard singing this epithalamium of love, while kissing his prison-chains:

'Soon, soon all the blood of my veins
Will be poured forth in copious streams.
My feet—oh what joy! are fettered with chains,
In bliss I await all my martyrdom's pains—
The sword of my torturer gleams!'

166St Thérèse: *Act of Oblation to Merciful Love.*

O quam gloriosum est regnum in quo cum Christo gaudent omnes sancti.[167]

Like this young martyr, there are so many saints—men and women—who burn with the desire of offering the supreme sacrifice, and for Whom the words of the great Apostle have become a living reality: 'For I reckon that the sufferings of this time are not worthy to be compared with the glory to come, that shall be revealed in us'.[168]

To be Thy prey, Oh Jesus! is not this the lot of every Carmelite, of every consecrated soul, whose vows and life of immolation make her Thy property and Thy victim? But she will only become such in the measure by which she makes Thy will her own—without drawing back; with faith, generosity and love—effective love, which sets no limit to the extent of the oblation once made.

'Because I love My Father, I do always the things that please Him', she should be able to repeat at every moment of the day. The divine will should be her food, her daily bread: she should allow herself to be immolated at the pleasure of the Father, as was the crucified Christ Whom she adores. Every occurrence, every event, each suffering, each joy is a sacrament which gives God to her so that she ceases to distinguish between them, but

[167]We have transcribed the following passage in its entirety, as it expresses so well that spirit of joy—one of the fruits of the Holy Ghost—flowing from the gift of Fortitude in souls. 'I await my sentence from day to day. One swift stroke will sever my head from my body, like the spring-flower which the gardener cuts for his own pleasure. Happy death, which leads to life! A little while, and then my soul will leave this earth, its exile will be over, its struggles finished. Soon I shall take my place under the banner of those who have been put to death for the sake of Jesus, and I shall sing the eternal Hosanna. But first, the grain of wheat must be ground, the bunch of grapes pressed. Shall I be bread and wine worthy to be tasted by the Father of the family? I hope so, through the grace of my Saviour and the assistance of His Immaculate Mother; and that is why, though still in the arena, I dare to intone the song of triumph as though I had already won the victor's crown'. (Last letter of Bl. Théophane Vénard to his father).

[168]Romans VIII, 18.

breaks through them and passes them by, to rest in God Himself above all else'.[169]

'I am ready to pass through fire, to do the will of God more perfectly'; declared Sister Elizabeth.[170]

Oh Jesus! Oh my Three! I wish to be Thy prey, Thy property, Thy Spouse, Thy victim, offering itself each day for the salvation of the world at the breaking of the Sacred Host, with Christ in the Holy Mass: *Suscipiat Dominus Sacrificium de manibus tuis, ad laudem et gloriam nominis sui ad utilitatem quoque nostram, totiusque Ecclesiae suae sanctae.*

Before receiving the Eucharistic Bread, the Priest divides it. Thus will it be for Thy little victim. Before absorbing her into the consuming sacrifice, Thou wilt break her, divide her, so that the holocaust may be perfect, pure, and acceptable to God.

Quid retribuam Domino? Calicem salutaris accipiam—What shall I render to the Lord? .... I will take the Chalice of Salvation— 'If I take this chalice, crimsoned with the Blood of my Master, and in joyous thanksgiving mingle my own blood with that of the sacred Victim Who gives it a share of His own infinity, it may bring wonderful glory to the Father. Then my suffering is a "speech" that utters the glory of the Eternal'.[171]

'Oh my Three, everything in me is Thine for ever—entirely at Thy disposal, whether for work or suffering—for the accomplishing of all Thy wishes and desires; for Thou art the Spouse of my life, and the Sovereign Master of my heart'. (Mgr Gay).

---

[169]*Heaven on Earth* 4th Day.

'According to the doctrine of great teachers like St Thomas, St Teresa and St John of the Cross, the soul is definitely established in the unitive life when she has no wilful attachment to anything; when her will is so entirely one with the divine will that she has no longer any will of her own. The union of the soul with God supposes the blending of two wills into one. From this time the soul no longer entertains, at least voluntarily, any personal or selfish feelings of joy, regret, fear or hope. She admits within her none but the thoughts and desires of God. Such are the conditions of the unitive life.' (Père de Jaegher: *One with Jesus*) p. 42.

[170]*Souvenirs.*

[171]*Last Retreat* 7th Day.

Seize upon Thy prey, then, without delay, oh my Three!
After having captured it so that it cannot wander out of Thy
radiance, bear it away to the highest heaven. Make it soar aloft,
borne on Thy eagle-wings, taken to Thyself.[172] In this infinite
solitude and unfathomable immensity, it will embrace Thy
omnipotence—and Thy great compassion for souls. Lost in
Thee, Thy desires will become more than ever its own, and like
little St Thérèse it will entreat Thee 'to cast Thy divine eyes on
a multitude of little souls, and to choose in this world a legion of
little victims worthy of Thy love.[173] Like her, it will know no
repose until the number of the elect is complete, until Thy glory
shall appear in the splendour of the eternal day: *Satiabor cum
apparuerit gloria tua*.... I shall be satisfied when Thy glory shall
appear'.

[172]Exodus XIX, 4.
[173]St Thérèse: *Autobiography*, Ch. XI.

141

BURY THYSELF IN ME, THAT I MAY BE BURIED IN THEE

We are buried together with Him by baptism unto death: that,
as Christ is risen from the dead by the glory of the Father,
so we also may walk in newness of life

(Rom. VI, 4)

THIS is the mystery of death which gives life. That the life of loving intimacy may be consummated here below, it is of vital necessity that one should bury oneself in the depths of the divine union, and lose oneself therein. Now it is only the dead that are buried. 'The mystic butterfly has died gladly, for she has found rest, and Christ lives in her'.[174] *The soul that desires to reach the heights must be dead to all created things, dead to itself, dead to its reputation, and its own concerns, dead to all that is not God and for His glory.*

'Oh God make us live as though dead, in a true and perfect Light', cried St Catherine of Siena. To arrive at this blessed death involves the whole process of the spiritual life—the upward climb, the night—and the Nights! The way that leads to God being 'so narrow that only a nothing can pass through it', the soul must at all costs become this 'nothing' in comparison with the 'All' of God, this 'nothing' fit to be engulfed within the changeless Immensity. 'Death is swallowed up in victory'. 'Oh death, I will be thy death', says the Lord. Oh soul, my adopted daughter, look on Me, and thou wilt lose sight of self: flow wholly into Me. Come, die in Me, that I may live in Thee'.[175]

Few souls, even among religious, are sufficiently faithful and generous to follow the Master as far as this. 'Can you drink of the chalice that I must drink.... *Potestis bibere calicem quem ego bibiturus sum?*'[176] Mysteries which only souls touched by Christ can perfectly understand, for the cross will always remain foolishness in the world's eyes.

[174]St Teresa: *Interior Castle*, 7th Mansion, Ch. III.
[175]Last Retreat 9th Day.
[176]St Matthew XX, 22.

From this supernatural death will spring life, fecundity, plenitude, unitive life, which can henceforth diffuse itself freely in action and in giving. From this life in God, one and Triune, dwelling in the soul which is wholly yielded up to Him, every grace will then spring as a ray from the interior Sun.

Oh my Three, bury Thyself in me, in peace and in beatitude!

'Henceforth in secrecy profound I dwell:
In life, in death buried within my Lord.
Grant me to sink into Thine endless peace—
I live but in Thy love, oh Word adored!'[177]

Oh my Three, my All! I am buried in Carmel for the sake of Thy love, Thou hast made me understand that I must bury myself there *in Thy love*, finding Thee unceasingly enclosed in the most intimate recesses of my being, in my interior heaven. I can in truth hide myself in the cleft of the rock, and repose under Thy shadow: *'sub umbra illius quem desideraveram sedi'*— For Thou dost cast Thy shadow over my path—translucent, embracing, enfolding.

In this divine atmosphere which surrounds me, everything speaks to me of Thee—everything leads me to Thee. It is the cloister of Thy love which keeps me ever separated from creatures, keeps me estranged from their disturbing movements —so futile when viewed from the supernatural angle.

Oh my Three! hold my soul the radiant captive of Thy love! Bear it away into the depths of Thy being where nothing can trouble it—unless on the surface—or distract it from Thee. There, *'I shall be led by Thy spirit; all that I do will partake of the divine, the eternal, and like Him Who changes not, I shall dwell here on earth in an eternal present'*.[178]

From this union of love will flow all activity, all work, prayer, suffering—purified in their motives and in their effects. I shall come to appreciate at its true worth 'the gift of God'.... I shall be the soul of prayer, who, seeing the harvest ripen prays unceasingly that the Father will send labourers—I shall be the

[177]*Poems of Sister Elizabeth.*
[178]Last Retreat 11th Day.

sower, letting fall only the good seed that has been selected by Thee—sifted by trial, temptation, complete immolation.

For I know that the life of a soul in this state is not repose, but work and suffering; urged by the interior force within her to undertake more than she can do, she wages a continual struggle against the body. But in vain does she take all these labours on herself—they seem a mere nothing to her in comparison with what she wishes to do and suffer for Thee, oh my Master.[179]

Ah yes! when the soul has arrived at the highest perfection, it only remains for it to consummate its sacrifice. This is accomplished more or less slowly—A secret torment devours it—the sight of Christ on the Cross, the memory of His profound humiliations, the thought of all He has suffered for its sake, are a continual torment. Then one day, a cry rends the heavens, a prayer demanding an answer, a suppliant cry: 'Either to suffer or to die: *Aut pati aut mori*—To suffer and to be despised: *Pati et contemni pro Te*'.[180]

[179]*cf.* St Teresa: *Interior Castle*, Mansion VII. Chap. IV.
[180]P. Servais: *Vie d'Espérance*.

UNTIL I DEPART TO CONTEMPLATE IN THY LIGHT THE ABYSS OF THY GREATNESS

Intra in gaudium Domini tui (Matt. XXV, 21)
A Praise of Glory is one who is always giving thanks
(Sister Elizabeth)

As we have already seen, this life of union is already the commencement of beatitude—heaven in faith—the heaven of pure love. *Habitamus et habitabimur*—'we shall dwell in God, and God in us'. (St Augustine). The soul which attains to this state is indeed profoundly happy; its ineffable joy is at the same time peaceful and unalterable, because it has its source in a total adhesion of all the faculties to the Divine Will.

'I am always happy, and always do just what I like', said the little saint of Lisieux, 'because I always will what God wills'. And Sister Elizabeth: 'Grow always in love. If you have something to suffer it is because you are still more loved. Love, and sing always: Thank you!'[181] There is the secret of the serene joy of a soul which is wholly surrendered. The obstacles which other souls may offer through self-love, immortification, caprice, do not exist for such a one. By a simple and trustful movement she betakes herself at once to the duty of the moment, as being the expression of the Father's will—manifested in the smallest details of daily life. For she knows that 'this Will ordains all things for its greater glory'; she surrenders herself to it, 'passionately, even to the point of being unable to desire anything except what God wills'.[182]

She adores this Will and embraces it, without questioning 'why' and 'how,' without delay, with all her heart, all her strength,[183] in the same manner, in fact as she loves God.

The act of loving surrender brings with it joy and reward. It is indeed the hundredfold promised in this life to the faithful servant—to the soul that surrenders and gives itself without

[181]Souvenirs.
[182]*Ibid.*
[183]Catechism. Act of Charity.

reserve, without recoil, utterly—seeing in all and through all, God present.

The life of such a soul is, as it were, a prelude to the life of heaven. She has a foretaste of the ineffable joy of the other world —the happiness of the elect, of the Virgins who follow the Lamb whithersoever He goeth, adoring Him with an eternal 'Amen'. [184] She tastes the fruit of pure love, which, according to St John of the Cross has three properties: fruition, praise, and gratitude, which resolve themselves into joy and peace.

In joy and in peace! It is there that I have fixed my abode, oh my Three—there, in Thy divine society, that I wish to sing unceasingly: there, in the deepest centre of my being, hymning Thy glory, that I long to make my life a triumphant cry of gratitude. May every note in this *Canticum Novum* by which I shall extol Thy glory, sing of thanksgiving! May all that is within me—prayer, work, silence, joy, zeal, self-oblation, sufferings, trials—give forth a harmony of joy and peace in a magnificent *Te Deum*, proclaiming Thy overflowing Goodness.

Is not this idea suggested in the realms of nature—where a wealth of gay flowers, diffusing their fragrant perfume, humming insects and light-winged birds, vast oceans and rippling streams, inaccessible heights and sheltering valleys, majestic trees, and grassy paths—all remind us that we are enclosed, so to speak, in the sweet embrace of that all-powerful Hand which orders and disposes all things sweetly, so that His creation unfolds and displays itself in a serene beauty.

We find the same thought again expressed in the paintings of the great Masters of the Renaissance;—an exuberance of life and colour, richness of tone, ample draperies and fullness of light, rhythmic form and a flame-like movement, which appear even

---

[184] 'Abound in thanksgiving. That is the last point of the rule and is but the consequence of the others. If you are rooted in Jesus Christ, confirmed in your faith, your life will be a constant thanksgiving, in the charity of the children of God. I wonder how a soul which has fathomed the love of God's heart for it, can ever be anything but joyful—whatever its sufferings or grief'. (Letter of Sr Elizabeth to a friend).

ın the least detail—and all this without jarring, in perfect harmony, exhaling joy and peace.

Then too, in the sound of bells, in the aerial concerts of towers and belfries, we find the same exuberance of life and joy pouring forth over sunny or cloudy skies harmonies alternately divine and human, light or thundering, but always ending in majestic calm.

So is it with a soul of thanksgiving—whether it prays, suffers, loves, works, gives itself in various ways—whether in trial or struggle, failure or success, in action or in contemplation, in exercises of devotion or in the repose of prayer, in vivid light or in a region of shadow, in joy or in sorrow—it is always the well-tuned instrument vibrating beneath the Hand of the Heavenly Father, in unison with the *Sanctus* of adoration offered to the divine glory.[185]

For a soul of thanksgiving is one who is always content with whatever God sends, withdraws, or puts to the test—with every thing that in one way or another is the expression of His Will. A soul of thanksgiving is one whose faith is so alive that it sees at once in a supernatural light every event and circumstance as coming from God, in whose wisdom and goodness it trusts with childlike simplicity and confidence.

It is one who is disposed to see the best side of everything—to perceive in everything a reflection of God's love—always ready to praise and sing the infinite mercies of the Lord.

A soul of thanksgiving is a profoundly happy soul, because it is established in faith and love. Considering this world only from the angle of eternity, it lives already the life of beatitude: *beatitudo inchoata*—which is a prelude through grace, to the unending happiness of the blessed in glory.

A soul of thanksgiving is strong with the strength of *God hidden*

[185]'When grace and love take possession of everything in our life,' said Dom Columba Marmion, 'our whole life becomes a perpetual hymn of praise to the glory of our heavenly Father. Through our union with Christ, it may be compared to a censer from which arise perfumes most agreeable to Him: *Christi bonus odor sumus Deo*'. (*Christ the Life of the Soul*, II Ch. 6).

within it, infusing into it unceasingly the gift of 'the strength of His right hand', giving it grace to achieve great things, to which humanly speaking, it could never hope to attain.

A soul of thanksgiving is one who is filled with Uncreated Wisdom, enlightened by Eternal Intelligence, in the knowledge of the ways of God. The gifts of the Spirit of love are reflected in and expand fully by praise and in praise.

In a word, a soul of thanksgiving is one who *lives in God and of God*, diffusing the superabundant and serene joy with which it is filled—radiating heaven.

Such a soul is truly a living praise of the glory of the Father, for it renders thanks continually to this Father of all sanctity, Who is pleased to 'hide these things from the wise and prudent and to reveal them to little ones.'

Oh my God, my Three! how many souls there are who weep, groan, and suffer without merit, because they are devoid of love and confidence. How many consecrated souls share in this weakening tendency through not living in Thee, with Thee, not suffering disinterestedly for Thee. How many souls are indifferent to Thy eternal designs, how many tepid ones, who never catch a glimpse of the supernatural horizons. Oh my God, would that we could offer in reparation for this incomprehension of the divine gift of the cross and of love, our poor life—as a victim of praise and thanksgiving! *Tibi sacrificabo hostiam laudis.*

Thou seekest hearts to console Thee: behold them here in Thy Carmels—hearts in which the life-giving breath of Thy all-embracing love creates perpetual spring-time. These souls offer Thee a radiant crown, woven of all the graces of detachment, crucifixion, darkness, light, peace of love, which Thou hast given; and sing Thy praises with the inspired canticles of Prophets and Saints'

> *Te Deum laudámus, Te Dominum confitemur....*
> *Laudate Dominum de caelis, laudate eum in excelsis....*
> *Benedicite omnia opera Domini Domino....*
> *Pange lingua, gloriosi Corporis mysterium....*

Oh my God!.... in the heart of a Carmelite there is always holiday—the mysterious descent of the Spirit. It is the 'glory of

the Lamb on the summit of Carmel'. It is the radiant joy which
Thou dost reserve for those who have 'stripped themselves' for
Thy sake.

Oh my Jesus! in this joy and outpouring of thanksgiving, we
wish to be for ever the Praise of Thy Glory.

A Praise of Glory in our physical powers surrendered to Thy
service, in our power to suffer, placed at the disposal of Thy
redemptive designs—

A Praise of Glory in our spirit filled with Thee—entirely ruled
and absorbed by Thy interests.

A Praise of Glory in our heart, united to Thine in perfect
conformity of will and love.

A Praise of Glory in our entire life, which will spread in a
hidden manner such a vibrant extension of Thy life on earth.

A Praise of Glory in our Soul, established in Thee, consecrated
to Thy love of predilection, unworthy recipient of the gifts and
immense graces of Thy Spirit, which until the day of our death,
we shall show forth in faith and in light, in renunciation and in
obedience, in devouring zeal.

Oh my God and my Saviour! in Thy 'Praise of Glory' thou
'wilt satisfy all Thy powers of loving; Thou wilt glorify the
Father'. In her and through her Thou wilt glorify Him unto
endless ages 'in the heritage of the saints, *in light*.[186]

---

[186]Colossians I. 12.

PRAYER TO OBTAIN THE BEATIFICATION OF SISTER ELIZABETH OF THE TRINITY

OH God, Who lovest souls so much as to make them Thy dwelling-place, we thank Thee for having enriched during her life on earth Thy humble servant Sister Elizabeth of the Trinity, by granting her a deep insight into this ineffable divine reality. If it should enter into Thy adorable designs to glorify with the honours of Holy Church her who longed to be even on earth the 'Praise of Thy Glory', deign we beseech Thee to show by external signs the favour she enjoys with Thee, to the end that she may extend the Kingdom of Thy love in souls, oh most Holy Trinity. Amen.